LEARNING TO FLY

Sam Keen

*Illustrations
by Jon Worden*

Broadway Books   New York

Learning to Fly

Trapeze – Reflections on Fear, Trust,
and the Joy of Letting Go

BROADWAY

Broadway Books titles may be purchased for business or promotional use or for special sales. For information, please write to: Special Markets Department, Random House, Inc., 1540 Broadway, New York, NY 10036.

BROADWAY BOOKS and its logo, a letter B bisected on the diagonal, are trademarks of Broadway Books, a division of Random House, Inc.

Library of Congress Cataloging-in-Publication Data
Keen, Sam.
    Learning to fly : trapeze—reflections on fear, trust, and the joy of letting go / by Sam Keen. — 1st ed.
      p.   cm.
    ISBN 0-7679-0176-2 (hc.)
    1. Keen, Sam. 2. Aerialists—United States—Biography. 3. College teachers—United States—Biography. 4. Acrobatics—Psychological aspects. I. Title.
    GV1811.K385A3   1999
791.3'4—dc21   98-50646
                                                       CIP

Visit our website at www.broadwaybooks.com.

FIRST EDITION

Designed by Keith MacLeod
Illustrated by Jon Worden

99   00   01   02   03   10 9 8 7 6 5 4 3 2 1

CONTENTS

I would believe only in a god who could dance. And when I saw my devil I found him serious, thorough, profound, and solemn; it was the spirit of gravity—through him all things fall. Not by wrath does one kill but by laughter. Come let us kill the spirit of gravity. I have learned to walk: ever since, I let myself run. I have learned to fly. Now I am light, now I fly, now I see myself beneath myself, now a god dances through me.

Friedrich Nietzsche

This book is dedicated to all who have helped me become a flyer and welcomed me into the airborne community.

For Tony Steele especially. One of the living legends, the first man ever to accomplish the triple-and-a-half somersault. He was my most frequent consultant on all matters technical and historical and, in the process, became a cherished friend.

For all my teachers from the San Francisco School of Circus Arts: Stephan Gaudreau, who founded the first program to teach flying trapeze to fledglings like me, Scott Cameron, Eric Vuillemey, Jorg Scott, Jennings McCown, Marek Kaszuba, Graham Day, and Aimee Hancock.

For the two anonymous angels who provided the rig and the support for the Upward Bound program.

For my fellow flyers in the Sonoma Trapeze Troupe, my daily companions at play.

A Philosopher in Midair

I didn't begin practicing the flying trapeze until two months before my sixty-second birthday.

But I always dreamed of flying.

The world I inhabited as a boy living in Boaz, Alabama; Maryville, Tennessee; and Wilmington, Delaware, was divided into quadrants—home, school, church, and woods.

Our home was rich in love, filled with music and biblical religion of a Calvinistic nature that made us more concerned with church and righteousness than with secular learning or success. Bible and prayer were daily bread, and on Sunday we sat together in the oak pew and listened to the preacher talking about the second coming of Jesus and the ascension of the chosen of the Lord. Ours was a three-story universe in which Heaven and Hell were more familiar than New York City. We lived in expectation of the apocalypse, had faith in the mercy of God, but worked diligently at being both orthodox in our beliefs and scrupulous in our morality.

School, I knew, was necessary but was not an arena in which I experienced either excellence or joy. It was only when I could escape to the woods that my spirit soared and I was free.

Trees, as every boy knows, are for climbing and getting

high, and my brother, Lawrence, and I made every effort to break the bonds of earth and live aloft. Even before we saw *Tarzan* or Kipling's *Jungle Book,* we knew that we were meant to be airborne. We searched out the trees along the creek that were hung with grapevines and learned to swing from tree to tree, finally falling into a thick mass of what we called pig-vines. When we tired of vines, we climbed to the top of nubile pines and rode the crests to the ground, hoping our weight would not snap the bowed trunks. I spent spellbound hours looking for indigo buntings and lying on my back watching changing cloud pictures. When it was time to go home we checked in and out as quickly as possible, took a supply of peanut-butter sandwiches, and adjourned to our tree houses in the far reaches of the backyard. When the rival neighborhood gang—the Long boys —began to threaten our castles in the trees, we spent our scarce dollars for hemp rope that we could climb, pull up, and be secure from attack. Once we found a large warehouse that was filled with cottonseeds, and before we were discovered and thrown out by the watchman, we climbed onto the highest rafters, jumped and fell into the gentle sea of seeds so many times that we began to feel at home in midair.

One mythic day in a time before I was counting my years, my father took us to the circus. I would like to tell you that I remember the big top, the peanuts, the balloons, the parade of elephants, the lion tamer, and the pratfalling clowns—I know they must have been there, but the truth is, I retain only one memory from that day, a single image so vivid that it has cast all others into an obscure background. I can see it still—I am sitting slightly to the left of the center ring, at an angle where I am looking up through the net. My hands are sweating as I watch the trapeze artists warming up. Then a flyer swings out over the crowd, reaches the high point of his arc, releases the trapeze, and . . . remains poised in midair. Logic tells me he must have been airborne for only a fragment of a second before he reached the hands of the catcher, but in my memory all action stopped and he was freeze-framed—a winged creature, a man in flight, free from the bondage of time and gravity.

The flying man soared into the center of my imagination and remained there. At the time, he seemed to be the furthest extension of everything I loved—trees for climbing, soaring birds, freedom from restraint—and I began to fantasize that someday I would be a trapeze artist. The day after the circus my brother and I went to the hardware store, bought a length of pipe and some rope, and rigged up our first trapeze from a tree in the front yard. Before the day was out we had swung so long that we developed mysterious pains in our stomachs, which Dr. Ellis assured our parents were nothing more than an occupational hazard of budding trapeze performers.

My first childhood ended in 1943 when the rope swings, the trapeze, and the life in the woods all disappeared, and we moved from Tennessee to Wilmington, Delaware, a city dominated by DuPont's promise of better things, for better living, through chemistry. My heart sank when I saw block after block of neat suburban houses and the mammoth high school in which I was to be incarcerated for six years, with its endless halls and rows of anonymous, olive-drab lockers. Even today I dream that I can neither find my locker nor remember the combination of the lock.

I felt imprisoned in the city. To the north, the oil refineries of Marcus Hook held high the eternal flame of modernity—the petroleum torch that burned off the excess gas and spewed noxious fumes into the surrounding air. To the east, across the river, a DuPont plant vomited a cloud of unknown particulates high into the air. Later, we discovered that the fallout from the cloud by day and the pillar of fire by night caused the emphysema from which my father died. Only westward did there seem to be any evidence of wilderness and freedom, and I found a thick woods with a stream where I could camp on weekends and sleep under the open sky. On the day I was to have attended my graduation, I loaded my camping gear into my Model A Ford and, with a friend, took off for the Wild West and the adventure of working on farms, ranches, and carnivals.

At summer's end in 1949, I returned and enrolled in Wesley Junior College. I didn't know what else to do. I got slightly better grades than the gentlemanly C+, but it was not until my senior year when I began to read philosophy that my mind caught fire. The spark was the Danish philosopher Søren Kierkegaard whose playful ways of thinking and writing about the great religious and ethical questions intrigued me. The tinder was my troubling questions about God, freedom, death, and sex, not necessarily in that order, and what I was to do with my life.

My questions led me to Harvard Divinity School where I began to experiment with different disciplines of mind, spirit, and body. I read the great philosophers and theologians, as if each might contain some secret message and speak directly to my condition. My mind became a symposium where I engaged in rich dialogue with the likes of Plato, Aristotle, St. Augustine, Nietzsche, Sartre, and the modern French philosopher Gabriel Marcel. Twice weekly I traveled across the Charles River to Boston University to take a course entitled "Spiritual Resources and Disciplines" with Dr. Howard Thurman, the philosopher and mystic who was to become my mentor and friend for three decades. Although I was immersed in the intellectual atmosphere of Harvard (where, one of my colleagues said, "We come to study religion, not practice it"), I was interested in experiential mysticism. In Dr. Thurman's class we experimented with prayer, poetry, silence, meditation, music, chanting, and the reading of inspirational texts. Twice weekly, I traveled to the Cambridge YMCA where I practiced the art of Olympic wrestling.

In retrospect, it is easy to see the schizophrenic assumptions that governed my life and my practice. One discipline for the mind, one for the spirit, one for the flesh—one labeled intellectual, one religious, and one sport—and never the three did meet. I was tough-minded in my studies, pious at prayer, and profane on the wrestling mat. It never occurred to me that the education of muscle, tendon, and sinew might be necessary to teach the spirit to soar. I was a captive of the prejudice against the body that has infected Western religion from its inception. Whereas the Eastern religions cultivate the marriage of flesh and spirit through the practice of yoga, aikido, tai chi chuan, archery, judo, and kung fu, the Western tradition has largely ignored bodily disciplines and divorced the quest for transcendence from sport and the muscular realm.

Although I did not understand it at the time, what appealed to me about the examined life and religious mysticism was not very different from the lure of the trapeze. All promised freedom, release from the mundane—a winged existence. It didn't take me long to discover that cultivating a questioning mind helped me break many of the chains of identity that had been forged by my parents and society, and that a playful imagination allowed me to explore a wide range of alternate lives.

One thing led to another in the long chain of my middle years. Graduate school led to a Ph.D., the sweet captivity of family life, a professorship in the philosophy of religion at Louisville Presbyterian Seminary, and a brick home on a shaded street. When an excess of homesteading began to do violence to the gypsy in me, I became troubled. Why was my spirit so heavy? Why was I so frequently depressed? So earthbound? So grave? So much of a somber Calvinist in spite of myself? I had worshiped long enough at the temple of Apollo. I longed for the freedom, the excess and ecstasy of Dionysius. Upon occasions I drank too much Kentucky bourbon, experimented with psychedelics, and danced out of control.

My inner journey led to new kinds of freedom, not all of them happy. When I went on sabbatical leave in 1969, the montage of normality exploded. On the spur of the moment, I resigned from the routine world of the professor and moved to California to pursue a career as a freelance writer and leader of workshops in Personal Mythology. A year later, for better and worse, the bonds of my marriage of seventeen years dissolved.

And, so it was, after emerging from the wilderness of the 1960s, that on a summer evening in 1976 I was swimming alone in a friend's pool, ruminating about my past and pondering the path ahead. I had recently remarried and my adolescent children were soon to be living with me. After a chaotic dozen years, things finally seemed to be settling down to something approaching orderly satisfaction. For the time being, I was tired of Dionysius. As I turned somersaults in the water, the flying man—whom I had not thought about for years—soared into my mind and I felt happy to have him back from the exile of deep memory. I laughed and addressed him. "Well, my young friend, you have come too late. I am too old for the circus. I will never fly through the literal air with the greatest of ease and know the joy of weightlessness. But I have learned something just as fantastic—the mind may become weightless and free. I have learned to think, to do all kinds of mental gymnastics—backward somersaults, passing leaps. I can contemplate daring possibilities and fall from high places without injury. I can consider most anything from multiple perspectives, jump from one side of an argument to the other with great dexterity. I can escape from ideological prisons and find my way out of blind alleys. I can destroy the systems erected by tyrannical authorities and dispel the illusion of false mysticism. I can wend my way into the secret places of a friend's heart and conjure up healing possibilities."

It was with a sense of quiet joy that I left the swimming pool that evening, having realized that I was content to be an artist in the circus of the mind . . . or so I thought.

CHAPTER 1

The Oldest Student
at the Circus School

Grow b/old gracefully.

Seventeen years later, in 1993, on an October evening, I was sitting comfortably at home flipping through the television channels and I heard the local news anchor say, "Did you ever dream of running away with the circus? Well, now you don't have to run away. Right after our commercial break we will take you on a visit to the first school where any more-or-less average person can learn the flying trapeze." Immediately, he had my undivided attention. The five-minute segment that followed reported that Stephan Gaudreau, a trapeze artist who had recently been performing at Circus-Circus in Reno, with the Flying Angels, had established a training program open to the public at the San Francisco School of Circus Arts.

The next Wednesday I went to the old gymnasium that housed the circus school to observe the beginners class and satisfy my curiosity. I was wearing a pair of tight Levis and a close-fitting shirt as I had no intention of participating. Stephan urged me to give it a try and assured me I would be in no danger; I would have a safety belt attached to lines the instructor held that would keep me from falling. From deep in the recesses of childhood, the flying man said, "Do it."

After warming up and hanging from a stationary bar for a

few minutes, I was fitted with a safety belt and pointed to a ladder that led to the trapeze platform. As I climbed and looked up, the thirty-one feet to the top of the rig seemed a long way. By the time I reached the platform and looked down at the net and the floor beneath, the distance had doubled and words like *abyss, chasm, void* came to mind. The primal fear of high places began to take me over. My hands began to sweat and adrenaline flooded my system. I had done enough rock climbing to know that the belaying rope would keep me from landing in the net in a dangerous way, and Stephan assured me "no one ever gets hurt in midair." Nevertheless, my stomach wasn't reassured. My heart was drumming as if I were a hapless Christian who had wandered into the wrong circus and was about to be fed to the lions.

I was in a daze. Everything was happening as if I were far away. Things were being said but I couldn't connect them to anything I was doing with my body. Stephan handed me the trapeze, told me to stand tall, lift it as high as I could, bend my knees, and ease my feet off the platform. I bent in exactly the wrong direction, trying to keep my butt well back in what felt like a secure position and still grasp the trapeze. Stephan said, "Ready. Hep," and I dove into the ocean of emptiness. My arms snapped like a bow that had suddenly broken a string, but the pain was brief and I was quickly lost in the pleasure of swinging—out and back, out and back.

The remainder of that first class went on forever and passed instantly. Since there were only two students, we climbed again and again to the platform. After a half-dozen tries I managed to stretch my Levis enough to creak the rusty hinges of my stiff body into an awkward knee hang, arch my back, and reach toward the catcher's trapeze. When the beginners class was finished, I stayed and watched the advanced class and saw much younger, but not impossibly talented, students doing tricks that seemed within my potential grasp.

That night after a hot bath and a couple of aspirin, I lay awake for a long time replaying the events of the evening in my mind. Every muscle in my upper body was sore. I knew about biceps and triceps but strange muscles in my back, shoulders, and stomach whose names I did not know were accusing me of abuse. I didn't exactly ignore the pain, but my mind was occupied with fantasies about the next class. If I stretched a bit more and wore flexible tights, I might be able to get into the knee hang a bit faster. Then I might be able to go to the catcher. I would be willing to suffer the outraged protest of a mass of muscles if, at my late age, I could fly for a brief moment. If I could accomplish the most elementary trick to the catcher, a knee hang in the safety lines, I would be satisfied.

The following Wednesday I showed up for the beginners class in new blue tights. I still mainlined a full dose of adrenaline each time I climbed the ladder and left the platform, but this time it didn't seem as if it was happening to somebody else. I worked on takeoffs and getting into the knee hang.

Midway in the class, the catcher showed up. One look was enough to give me confidence that, if we could make hand contact, he would not drop me. All those unknown muscles that had announced their presence to me the previous week were old friends of his. He looked like Superman without a shirt. He climbed hand over hand up the rope without using his feet, perched on the catcher's trapeze, and began to build up his swing. He dropped to his knees and pulled himself over into the catcher's lock with his legs entwined in the ropes and shouted, "Ready." When he reached the apex of his arc he yelled, "Hep."

I lifted the trapeze and took off from the platform, but I got into the knee hang too late to meet him at the midpoint. No catch.

The second time I folded myself as tightly and quickly as

possible, hooked my knees around the bar, took my hands off, and reached for the catcher. It happened.

Suddenly, out of nowhere, out of the kingdom of the flying man, the catcher appeared. As he grasped my wrists, I released my knees from the bar and we flew out over the apron, over the crowd, over the years, and swung back again. He released me and I fell into the net, and into my dream.

That night I hardly slept. I don't remember anything about muscles or fatigue. Only elation. Time and again I saw myself on the trapeze going to the hands of the catcher, and sometimes it was me and sometimes it was my ancient twin, the flying man. It had been easy for me to entertain the fantasy of flying but I couldn't believe in the reality. I had gone beyond the limits of the possible. I had done in fact what I assumed I could do only in imagination.

That might well have been the end of it. Common sense would suggest I should count myself fortunate to have been able to fulfill a childhood fantasy; I should tuck the whole affair away safely in my album of memories. Instead, I listened to some whispered hope that came from deep within or beyond myself, some echo from a realm that promised I had been created to soar, to transcend, to know the joy of flying.

So, although I was content with my accomplishments, my imagination began to beguile me with the notion that I might go one step further into the impossible dream. With a bit of practice I might make the journey from trapeze to catcher and back to the swinging trapeze.

The following Wednesday I attempted the return from the catcher three times and managed to touch but not hold on to the bar.

The following Wednesday (by now you may rightly suspect a liturgical repetition), I flew to the catcher, swung back, tightened every muscle, screwed my resolve to breaking point, and hurled myself across the void toward the trapeze—with a lot of help from the man pulling the safety lines. My forearms slammed against the bar, but somehow I slid down, grasped it, and hung on.

Wednesday followed Wednesday for a few months before the craving to fly grew stronger and began to consume my Saturdays and establish a beachhead on the other days of the week. With a little work I managed to jerry-rig a trapeze and a makeshift pedestal in a tree on my farm so I could swing, limber up, get my arms and shoulders in shape, and practice the basic positions—knee hang, bird's nest, and plange—any time the notion hit me.

The dream had become a passion.

My emerging passion was not unlike falling in love, a bit of ecstasy and a lot of foolishness. In what should have been idle moments I found myself tracing and retracing the configurations made by flying bodies as they move through the positions necessary to accomplish a layout or a plange. When I tried to sleep, my mind turned tricks. In polite social gatherings I was apt to describe the intricacies of my latest move on the trapeze, like a late-blooming man newly awakened to the erotic arts who insists on recounting his explorations of the positions for lovemaking. I was all too happy to detail the over, the under, the in and out of it all to anyone who would listen. At first, casual acquaintances and friends alike were fascinated by my stories, but after a while, I noticed their eyes began to glaze, and when they finally escaped they no doubt shook their heads and muttered, "Strange passion!"

Strange passion, indeed. But then, all passions are strange to those who do not share them. The passions that animate individuals thrive in the most unexpected nooks and crannies. There are people who are ecstatic about collecting stamps, old motorcycles, or vintage Levis. Or painting pictures of barns. I know otherwise normal people who are wildly enthusiastic about riding around on manicured lawns in electric carts and hitting little white balls into holes in the ground. I have met numerous cabdrivers who can't keep their checkbooks balanced but can give you the batting average of everyone who ever played in the World Series. And many a man has kept the smell of the salt sea in his nostrils while building a sailboat in a backyard in Iowa.

During the first months of my blossoming love affair I had to contend with all the "sensible" critical voices from within: "Don't you think you are a little old for this? Trapeze artists usually begin training in their teens and retire by the time they are forty."—"You're dyslexic and can't even learn the tango, so you certainly are never going to be any good at dancing in midair."—"Grow up. Act your age. Devote your energies to something more socially useful. It's time for you to be a mentor and give moral guidance to the young, not be playing around with a ridiculous fantasy." All true, but somehow beside the point.

Passion is seldom rational and usually blind. You can bet that when you are suddenly swept away—abandon your marriage, take a new lover, quit your job, buy a sailboat, run off with the circus—in due course you will discover that the overt object of your affections is a surrogate for covert longings that you hide even from yourself. Over the years I have discovered that it is hazardous to ignore passing fantasies and emerging passions.

To begin with, in the degree that I cease to pursue my deepest passions, I will gradually be controlled by my deepest fears. When passion no longer waters and nurtures the psyche, fears spring up like weeds on the depleted soil of abandoned fields. I suspect that the major cause of the mood of depression and despair and the appetite for violence in modern life is the result of the masses of people who are enslaved by an economic order that rewards them for laboring at jobs that do not engage their passion for creativity and meaning.

It is from the unlikely region of the psyche where fantasy is king, a realm still governed by the logic and desires of childhood, that renewal comes. There is a time and a place for hard work, tough-minded realism, rational and moral seriousness, and mature commitments. I have happily paid my dues to these virtues. But, roughly every decade, I have become stale and bored with good habits and domestic routines. Several times I plunged down the slippery slide toward depression until I learned to pay attention to the "frivolous" and "unrealistic" fantasies playing at the edge of my awareness. Each time I respected and nurtured my fantasies some new passion emerged, an underground spring bubbled to the surface, watered the parched ground, and brought new forms of vegetation to life.

According to the late Renaissance Swiss physician Paracelsus, all things are composed of four elements—water, fire, earth, and air—and the human soul in its pilgrimage through time must inhabit and bring into harmony all the elements of which the cosmos is constructed.

I came to know elemental water during my twenties and thirties when I was immersed in exploring the life of the mind, first in graduate school, then as a professor of philosophy and religion. During these years, I was a passionate and accomplished scuba diver, addicted to the thrill of escaping altogether from the pull of gravity. I developed a quicksilver mind that could not be stopped by orthodoxies and dogmas but flowed with the currents of my own experience as easily as I glided, weightlessly, beneath the ocean. I learned to dissolve false dilemmas, to deconstruct rigid systems that kept mind and body imprisoned in lockstep alternatives. When my own inherited beliefs, values, and self-images fell apart, I dove deep into the dark waters of the unconscious and learned to swim in that underground river of image, fantasy, and feeling where there is no before and no after.

Approaching forty, I abandoned academic philosophy but continued the overexamined life of a writer until I felt something within me drying up and becoming brittle. Needing to come to ground, to know my own earthiness, I bought a small farm on the trailing edge of the Cascades and learned something of the ways of the soil and growing things and fulfilled my childhood fantasy of riding horses through wide open country.

More than once I have been tempered by fire, not always without burning myself and others who were caught up in my quest. The fire and folly of affairs of the heart, or other organs, have enlivened and impoverished me, sometimes resulting in a warm hearth and sometimes in third-degree burns. At long last, I am mostly convinced that errant sexual passions are a substitute for exploring the undiscovered passions that are buried in the terra incognita of the self. Freud taught us that rigid moralism was often a sign of repressed sexuality. He failed to warn us that sexual obsession is often a sign of repressed spirituality. Sex may be a substitute for the kind of release and freedom we find in flying.

In my sixties I face a new set of challenges. Like the god Janus, I face two directions. Looking backward, I take a measure of satisfaction in what I have accomplished and learned of water, earth, and fire. Looking forward toward the ripeness of my years, I know I must avoid the folly of grasping and trying to keep a stranglehold on my fleeting days. If I get stuck in who I am now, I will never blossom into who I might yet become. Today's identity is tomorrow's prison. I need to practice the gentle art of surrendering and letting go. It is time for me to inhabit the air, to learn to move more gracefully and effortlessly.

I am not certain where this unlikely fascination with flying leads or what it signifies. There are times when it is wise to tie yourself to the mast and resist the siren's song; and other times when following them is the only way home. All I know for certain is that I am being beckoned, and that at the core of my being there are good, if mystical, reasons known only to my inarticulate heart for persisting in this strange behavior.

I feel as if I have been thrown into the middle of a mystery story and have received a message in a fortune cookie: ''Return to the setting—the circus—where you first saw the flying man and you will find the next clue about how you should proceed.''

CHAPTER 2

The Cosmic Circus

Come to the big top with me. Children of all ages come into the hippodrome, the carnival, the sacred saturnalia. Unless you become a little child you will never enter the Kingdom of Wonders, never travel beyond the physical to the metaphysical.

Once inside the tabernacle, appearance and reality turn topsy-turvy, the impossible becomes possible, the profane becomes sacred, and vice versa.

Wild animals are more docile than teenagers. Tigers snarl but obediently sit on their perches and jump through burning hoops upon command. Elephants stand on their heads. Monkeys dressed as children stroll around the arena.

Lions lie down with lambs.

Dogs jump through hoops. Goats walk tightropes. Liberty horses wheel and turn with the precision of the Rockettes.

Men and women dance and jump along a high wire, ride a unicycle across an abyss.

A cannon fires, but instead of a warhead, a human projectile flies across the arena and lands safely in a net.

Characters straight out of fairy tales appear out of nowhere—giants and midgets, beautiful women and handsome men on white horses.

Bearded ladies, wolf men, alligator boys, Siamese twins, half-men–half-women—"freaks" of nature inhabit their separate kingdom on the edge of the midway.

Clowns in outlandish costumes gleefully shatter the shell of normality, purposely create pandemonium. A miniature car rolls up and contrary to all expectation seventeen people emerge from it. A policeman saunters up and is hit in the face with a pie. A fire truck rushes in and squirts water everywhere except on the fire. The arena gets so slippery that everyone is falling over each other. A fight erupts and everyone ends up flat on their backs.

And then comes the finale, the diamond in the setting of impossible possibilities—the flying trapeze. High above the circus arena, men and women cavort in midair with bodies so light they seem to soar beyond the human condition and break free from the tyranny of gravity.

The whole thing—three rings or one—makes our heads spin. The circus overwhelms us with improbable spectacles. It scrambles our categories. What is going on here? What kind of drama is being enacted in this theater of incarnate dreams? What kind of sacrament is being celebrated in this church of impossible possibilities?

What kind of weltanschauung are we to deduce from this variety show of the spirit?

Only this is clear. Entering the circus we step back into a world ruled by enchantment—where magic existed before morality, wonder before worship, pleasure before piety, and amazement before practicality.

The atmosphere of the sawdust arena is not the dour aesthetic of the zendo or the hushed piety of the church, where laughter is rare and the ego is declared the enemy of wisdom and compassion. The activities—the liturgies of the circus—are as impractical as prayer and as demanding as Zen archery, but the mood in which they are performed is quite different. It takes a special kind of fool to spend a lifetime honing a useless skill—juggling balls, taking pratfalls, or teaching elephants to dance. In the circus, ego is center stage. The actors are not shy or retiring. Each performer seeks to capture the eyes of the audience and win its applause. Like a child, the lion tamer asks us to praise his skill and daring. After each trick, the trapeze artist throws his arms wide in a gesture of styling, bows, invites the audience to admire and celebrate a worthy performance.

When the last act has finished and we walk out of the circus tent, we shake our heads, still unable to believe what our eyes have seen. Under the spell created by the catharsis of laughter and awe, we are transubstantiated, transformed, changed back into children whose horizons are open.

The circus, like philosophy, invites us to question our normal judgments. The dilemma is as old as Lao Tzu, the Chinese philosopher who dreamed he was a butterfly and then wondered: "Am I a man dreaming I am a butterfly or a butterfly dreaming I am a man?" Am I a dense body dreaming of the impossible freedom of flying, or an airborne spirit incarnate in a world of wonders? Is my ultimate destiny dust to dust or breath to breath?

This so-called universe seems to be some kind of divine drama, an intricate game, or a ten-ring circus, and I am Everyman trying to escape from being earthbound. The circus is a visible mystery play that holds up a mirror in which I see a reflection of my invisible soul. I dreamed of flying long before I ever saw a trapeze.

The circus is good for you. It is the only spectacle I know that
while you watch it gives the quality of a truly happy dream. . . .
The flyers catch each other the way you are caught in good dreams.

Ernest Hemingway

When my daughter Lael was very small, she developed
an unshakable conviction that she could fly. For weeks she
talked about how she would do it, before she began to practice
by jumping from the lowest limb on the dogwood tree in the
front yard. When she crashed to the ground several times, she
reasoned that she needed some lighter-than-air substance to
buoy her up. On that terrible morning when she was cast out
of the Garden of Eden, she came into the house with skinned
and bleeding knees and explained to us between heartbroken
sobs that she had taken a small piece of very thin tissue paper,
placed it between her fingers, and jumped from the highest
limb she could reach.

If her hope was naive, it is nevertheless a universal dream
that is ingrained in human nature and is expressed in many
forms. The history of religions is filled with the symbolism of
ascension and flight. The gods have always lived in high
places—on hills and mountains and in the heavens. The soul's
journey is to the holy hill, the mountaintop, the high heavens.
Yogis, sages, mystics, sorcerers, and shamans have always
claimed the magical power to leave their bodies at will and fly
into regions inaccessible to the living. What are angels but
flyers given feathers and wings by our imaginations, inspirited
bodies not bound by the constraints of time, space, or gravity?

The fundamental reason our hands sweat when we watch a
flyer leave the trapeze is because we all yearn to fly. We are

creatures of longing. We do not need to climb the long ladder to the pedestal or grasp the fly bar to be airborne. What I call the aerial instinct—the drive to transcend our present condition—is *the* defining characteristic of a human being. We are restless animals, eternal travelers who are forever in the process of becoming. Consciousness itself is a flight from the here and now and to the beyond. Our reach always exceeds our grasp, which is what heaven is for—and the circus. Deeper than any skepticism, we nourish the hope that when we are freed from the limits of time and space we will fly away home, even though we have less than a vague notion of what that might mean.

When we visit the circus or inhabit our dreams, we make contact with the primordial self that longs to let go and be free, to live gracefully within the limits of gravity and mortality. The shamanic power of magical flight is still present in each of us and invites us to take the journey into our dreams, into the mythic reality of flight.

My earliest childhood dreams of flying were mostly marred by images of falling. Everything was dark and I was falling down, down, down, through endless space inside something like a deep grave. Was it the hell that awaited all whom God had not chosen to save or the pit of death that lurks beneath existence that frightened me? I don't know. Anxiously, I awaited the fearful moment when I would hit bottom. But I never did. Just before the crucial moment I would wake up breathless and sweating.

By the time I reached my teens, I had learned a little about soaring. The wind would lift me and carry me swirling through the clouds and I enjoyed being a plaything of the currents, until I realized with a shock that I was completely out of control of my life. My moods fluctuated wildly. I had no idea how to pilot my mind or emotions. The winds of my fate—my unconscious, my persona—took me in a direction that was often alien to my will. Neither boy nor man, I was fearful of flying too high on my new wings because I had no confidence in my ability to land safely.

It was not until I awakened to sex and began to break free of the religious and sexual dogmas I had inherited that I first experienced ecstatic flight in my dream body. I still remember that first flight as vividly as I remember my first sexual dream. The wind whisked me high into the air over the tapestry of Pennsylvania farmland. Far below me were recently harvested fields, lakes and barns, and houses small enough for dolls. When I realized how far above earth I was soaring, I became frightened and started to plummet. Instinctively, I took a large breath to prepare myself for a hard landing. But to my surprise, the breath acted like an infusion of helium in a balloon that stopped my fall and caused me to rise ever so gently. It was then that I realized I could control my flight by the volume of air I inhaled and exhaled. Breathing in and out I soared with the wind, swooping low over the earth and rising up into the clouds. As I experimented with this newfound ability to control my flight, I realized that I was, for the first time in my life, dreaming in color. The farms and woods beneath me were painted in vivid autumn colors. I had burst out of a gray world into full Technicolor. My fear of falling was being transformed into the joy of flying.

As I became proficient at flying in my dreams I noticed a corresponding sense of freedom and personal power. I began to trust more in my own sense of purpose and direction and take greater delight in who I was discovering myself to be. The opinions and judgments of others swayed me less, and I acted with greater verve and interior certainty. I broke the chains of habits and obsessions that had held me for years and ceased to eat the rancid daily bread of old fears.

I discovered, as had the philosopher Friedrich Nietzsche, the power of the dream to transform daily life. In *Beyond Good and Evil,* he wrote:

What we experience in dreams belongs in the end just as much to the over-all economy of our soul as anything experienced "actually." Suppose someone has flown often in his dreams and . . . he is conscious of his power and art of flight as if it were his privilege, also his characteristic and enviable happiness. He believes himself capable of realizing every kind of arc and angle simply with the lightest impulse; he knows the feeling of a certain divine frivolity, an "upward" without tension and constraint, a "downward" without condescension and humiliation—without gravity! *How could a human being who has had such dream experiences and dream habits fail to find that the word "happiness" had a different color and definition in his waking life, too? How could he fail to— desire happiness differently?*

Last night I dreamed I was flying on the trapeze. All my movements were fluid and graceful. It seems my dream body has a sacred wisdom that is still hidden from my conscious mind.

My passion and dreams excite me with a promise of levity. Do they lead to fulfillment or folly? Are they the promptings of heavenly or demonic eros?

My condition is this. I know I am nearsighted. I am imprisoned within a psyche that limits my vision. Everything that clusters around my name and my identity keeps me from seeing what is beyond my ego. No matter how hard I try, I can't jump out of the parenthesis of my own time and space. Sometimes, I am comfortable enough in my little cocoon. It is cozy in here and secure. I'm well-off, and even well thought of by my contemporaries.

But, at times, I am troubled by a feeling that is an amalgam of longing, curiosity, and dread, because even though I am horizon-bound, I know I am encompassed by a great Beyond. Even when I feel most solitary, I know that I am within some Web of Being that is infinitely larger than myself. Sometimes I feel like a spectator watching Salome's dance of the seven veils. No sooner does she take off one veil than I see the next. For all I know there may be an infinite number of veils, but I am hypnotized by the dance, excited to be in the presence of the Mystery, and don't want to leave the theater.

This agnosticism about the great Mystery within which I live and move and have my being would not be troubling if only I could resign myself to the condition of ultimate ignorance. Then I could settle down and decorate my cocoon with all the latest items that are guaranteed to bring me happiness. I could take seminars on self-esteem, buy a cappuccino machine, and hook up to the Internet.

Some urge, some instinct, keeps driving me to transcend my encapsulation. I have a completely unverifiable feeling that something in my DNA has destined me to become a butterfly. I am programed to escape from this cocoon, to fly in the direction of the Beyond, but I neither know how to fly nor do I know the route. I imagine myself like a monarch butterfly just emerging from the cocoon who must soon set forth on a migration of thousands of miles over uncharted mountains and seas. I can only hope that some inner compass will guide me on the journey.

All of this brings me back to my ancient dreams of flying and my strange passion for trapeze. I have a hunch that they contain metaphysical clues I need to decipher.

Dr. Freud taught me that the first thing to do when I come across any "highly cathected" (or numinous) event, memory, or fantasy that seems to be a clue to something deeper is to free associate. I can also hear Sherlock Holmes prompting me, "Elementary, my dear Watson," follow the trail that begins with the notion of "flying." What is it that animates a man who suddenly becomes obsessed with a dream of flying? If a man passionately desires to fly, to soar, to be airborne, to levitate, to escape from gravity, it must be because such a person feels himself, at heart, to be too earthbound, too heavy, too dense, too serious, too grave.

I am captive to the laws of gravity, condemned to death by the second law of thermodynamics. My life cycle is no cycle at all but a path that ascends till midlife and then turns downward. Time drags me toward the humus. If I discover the secret of levity maybe I can break free, for one marvelous instant, from the bonds of time, the limits of the past, and the pull of gravity.

For the moment, this diagnosis gives me something to go on, a glimpse into the obscure ground of my motivation, a splinter of understanding of my quest.

I am not alone in this need for levity. There is something ominous, heavy, and deadly serious in the air these days. The most modern of us have become grave, self-important, and obsessed with work. A generation ago, Herbert Marcuse predicted that the "problem" of the 1990s would be "the leisure revolution." We would all have to work only twenty hours a week and we wouldn't know what to do with our free time. Instead we have become captives, driven by the demands of our corporations, the market economy, and the pressures of globalization, which exist side by side with the escalating violence caused by tribalism, nationalism, and anarchy. It is a hot and heavy world. Not much joy in high places. Our humor is confined to comedy clubs and sitcoms. A lighthearted competitor never wins the fair maiden, or the large bonus.

We are in the grip of the spirit of seriousness, which Nietzsche equated with the devil. "When I saw my devil I found him serious, thorough, profound, and solemn; it was the spirit of gravity—through him all things fall."

In the biblical myth, Lucifer, son of the morning star, fell and became the Prince of Darkness because he was too upwardly mobile. He wanted to be Number 1. The "dark side of the force" is an enemy of skywalking, laughter, and levity.

I set forth on this adventure with the hope that I will meet the Prince of Lightness, be inspired by the spirit of levity, and become en-lightened.

CHAPTER 3

Becoming a Connoisseur of Fear

It is a poor life in which there is no fear.

Aldo Leopold

During my *first year* of practice I was
acutely aware of an alternating current of fear and fascination
that pulsed through my body each time I approached the trapeze. An hour before a session, as I was driving from my home
in Sonoma to the San Francisco School of Circus Arts, I would
imagine the tricks I was going to practice and my pulse rate
would gradually rise. Once in the gym, I would go to the
stone-cold bathroom and put on my tights. No sooner was I
dressed than I had to move my bowels. Like any wild animal
sensing danger, I automatically prepared for fight or flight.

By the time I had finished my warm-up and climbed to the
pedestal, a tide of adrenaline coursed through my system and
turned my body into a high-tension electrical wire. My fear was
raw and brutal. A thundering herd of terrors stampeded
through the canyons and plains of my body. My heart beat
wildly; my chest constricted and my breath came in rapid,
shallow bursts; my eyes flitted in every direction trying to identify the source of the threat; my legs shook. The hoofbeats
came closer and began to trample my mind and destroy my
reason. The voices in my head said, "I am afraid of high places.
Afraid of falling. Afraid of getting hurt." I looked into the void,

vertigo assaulted me, and an urgent voice warned me, "Get out of here, get back onto solid ground before something terrible happens."

But at the last minute, always the last minute, something in me refused to flee before the onslaught, refused to yield to the blackmail of catastrophic expectations. I repeated as a liturgy the advice of the Persian poet Rumi, "Do not go the way fear bids you to go." I stood my ground, turned around, and looked at my fears with cool eyes.

After one session in which I had repeatedly attempted a new trick and had vibrated all evening as if I had drunk too much espresso, I returned home, took a hot bath, drank a brandy to help me come down from my elevated state of excitement, and tried to think calmly about my experience of the last months.

The practice of trapeze has acquainted me with many unholy ghosts that hide in the dark regions of the psyche.

There is nothing mysterious about the simple survival fears that warn us against the dangers of frolicking around high places. There are only three fears that are instinctual for human beings: the fear of falling, the fear of being imprisoned in a tight space, and the fear of loud noises. So, it is pure biological wisdom that warns me that soaring on the trapeze is apt to result in pain, injury, or death and that I should be especially careful since I am no longer young and nimble.

There is a deeper level of psychological fears that is connected with self-image and is rooted in unconscious feelings of shame and guilt. Both in myself and in others I have noticed that once the fear of literal dangers has been mastered, a more complex fear of symbolic dangers emerges. I am afraid of failure. I am afraid of what others will think of me. I am afraid I will embarrass myself. I am afraid I will lose control. I am afraid I can't trust you. I am afraid I will be abandoned if I do not measure up to your expectations. I remember one dramatic instance in which a young woman peeled away layer after layer of her fears over a four-day period. Thin to the point of being undernourished, her body permanently bent into the shape of a question mark, on the first day she remained silent and refused to participate. The second day she forced herself to climb a few rungs of the ladder but was too frightened of high places to go more than six feet above the ground. The third day she announced that she wanted to climb to the pedestal but asked if someone would climb with her. I encircled her with my arms and climbed step by step with her. Every few feet she stopped and verbalized her feelings: "I am afraid you will let me fall. I am afraid I can't trust you." I tightened my arms and reassured her that she was safe. After another few feet she began to cry softly through her shaking. "My father walked out on the family when I was twelve years old, and I have never seen him since. I am afraid you will abandon me." When we got near to the top of the ladder, she paused for a long time and described how the entire world around her was spinning and coming apart at the seams. We descended step by step. The next day, she told me that during the night she had awakened from a dream in a state of terror and had been flooded with memories of being sexually abused by her father. An hour later she asked if everyone in the group would gather around the base of the ladder while she climbed to the pedestal. Unassisted, she climbed and was welcomed at the top by one of the instructors. For ten minutes she hesitated, struggling to get the courage to make her maiden flight. Finally, with a scream of fear and exaltation, and loud applause from the group, she launched herself into the face of her fears. When she climbed down from the net, it was clear to everyone that she was a new being.

Beneath our fear of high places and things that go bump in the night, there is a primal fear, what the existentialists called ontological anxiety—the fear of extinction, of the void, of nothingness, of death—that is an abiding climate in the bottom of the psyche.

Since fear is such a complex phenomenon, it creates illusion and unhappiness in so far as we allow it to remain unconscious. If we fail to separate, classify, decipher, and demystify our various fears, they appear in disguised forms.

For instance. When I was younger and more macho, I habitually denied my fears and they sidled out under the guise of braggadocio and false courage. "The difficult I do immediately, the impossible takes a little longer." These days, when age has fatigued and mellowed me, they are much more apt to appear as a passive-aggressive whiner who makes excuses. "I'm sleepy. I'm too tired. I feel a little bit sick today."

The other day all of the disguises fell away long enough for me to see the unadorned face of my deepest fear.

I was experimenting with getting into a position on the trapeze from which I could drop face first into the net. I swung off the pedestal, flipped into a knee hang, and swung back and forth several times, but was not comfortable in letting go. As I flipped back into a full hang, I felt dizzy from a too rapid transition from head-down to head-up, and . . .

The next thing I knew, I was awash in a tingling sea of warmth with no awareness of who or where I was or what had happened to me. I saw a shadow passing back and forth in front of my eyes. As my vision cleared I saw it was the trapeze swinging over my head. I had fainted, fallen, and was lying on my back in the net. My first thought was "this is what death is like, suddenly you just aren't there anymore." Then I realized that, this time at least, I had been resurrected immediately.

The minideath left me shaken. I wasn't overly concerned with the actual fainting, because it was due to a simple mistake

I would not repeat of going too rapidly from upside down to right side up. But the momentary oblivion, the total self-loss, the encounter with nothingness threw me into a state of vague anxiety.

That evening when I lay in bed, all the stories—of flyers who have broken arms, legs, necks, who have been killed by falling wrong in the net—ran through my mind, time and again, constricted my heart, and made me timid. I wanted to cower under the covers where it was safe. A voice pretending to be the voice of wisdom warned me to avoid all unforeseen dangers.

What, I wondered, is this black hole into which everything disappears, all courage, all resolve, all rationality? It is unlike my ordinary fear with which I can negotiate and that sometimes I can conquer. This one is older than my psyche and larger than my ego. In an effort to learn the name of the monster, I curled into the fetal position and allowed myself to sink into the feeling of pure panic. Gradually, a voice, almost a whisper, emerged from the black hole. "I am small, alone, sad, and helpless. Death is lurking. My only hope is to curl up, be very still, and wait. I am abandoned. Please rescue me."

Holding the deadly fear in my hand (like a surgeon holding a diseased heart), I discovered that it has always been with me since the earliest days of my childhood. It lurks like a virus just beneath the surface of my awareness. It is a driving force. It causes me to approach my life as if I had to escape from some danger each day; it puts a slight pall of dread over everything. If I could take a slice through all the levels of my consciousness at any moment and put it under the microscope, I would find that anxiety about existence is like a dye that suffuses and colors all experience. Anxiety—low-grade fear—is a primal motive force. In the degree that I remain unconscious of its presence, it drives me to strive for impossible fulfillment, makes me dissatisfied with any achieved goal, impels me to prove myself before a spectral audience, work and be virtuous in order to earn the approval of an absent God. It destroys my contentment and steals away my simple pleasures.

Now I understand the folly of trying to defeat this demon! Like squaring the circle, it is not to be done. My temptation to panic is rooted in a primal sense of abandonment, in my final helplessness in the face of the vastness of the cosmos and the threat that in death I will be swallowed up into nothingness.

How do I deal with this metafear—death, nothingness, the void? The question is philosophical or religious, not psychological. I do not have any firm religious belief in immortality, resurrection, or reincarnation although I do have a kind of agnostic trust in the nameless One that birthed me into being. How do I acquire what my old professor at Harvard, theologian Paul Tillich, called "the courage to be" that allows me to exist creatively with my fear? More than this. How can I be joyful when my final fall is to the grave?

This much is clear to me. I do not believe I can ever conquer fear, and I suspect those forms of spiritual heroism that claim to banish it. St. Paul advised us that love casts out all fear, but then Paul had neither wife nor children nor friends who were exceptionally close and irreplaceable. If one breaks all intimate attachments to other persons, by definition, one does not fear losing other persons. But in the measure that I love and hold dear my father, my mother, my brother and sisters, my children, my wife, and my friends, I fear their possible loss and grieve their actual loss. Nor do I accept the Eastern doctrine of detachment. Eugen Herrigel's classic book, *Zen in the Art of Archery,* which is based on the notion that the warrior is the ideal human type, explains that the sword master "no longer knows what fear of life and terror of death are. He lives . . . happily enough in the world but ready at any time to quit it without being in the least disturbed by the thought of death. . . . He is no longer capable of experiencing what fear feels like.'' Perhaps I am not spiritually advanced enough to have given up attachments and acquired the virtue of fearlessness.

There is a small dialogue that takes place between a flying master and his new students that is one of the standard litanies of the tribe: "Are you afraid?" the master asks.

"Yes, I am," the student replies.

"Good," the master responds. "I would be worried about you if you were not."

Even professional flyers retain a lively and realistic respect for the dangers of their trade and a measure of appropriate fear. Isabel Caballero, a flyer with the Flying Caballeros and one of the handful of women currently performing the triple somersault, told me, "Even after all these years I am afraid all the time. Every time I climb up on the pedestal I look down and I think about how high up it is. But I love flying more than I fear it." This professional aerialist's subtle relationship to fear echoes the sentiment expressed by the legendary Alfredo Cadona, "We fear falling. But we do not fear that we will fall."

The real question is not "Are you afraid?" but what are you fearful of and what do you do with fear? Some people are afraid of embarrassing themselves by their clumsiness and refuse to try to fly. Some are afraid of climbing the ladder. Some are afraid of falling from high places only when they get to the pedestal and look down. One woman with whom I sometimes practice is so afraid of failure that she curses herself violently whenever she doesn't do a trick "perfectly." Two of my flying companions, David and Kat, who are both more daring than I in trying new tricks, are afraid they are not strong enough to hold on and might slip off the bar. I have the grip of a bulldog and I have no fear of a failure of strength, but I am afraid of the net. I am not flexible and I don't trust myself to turn in midair and land in a safe position.

And, all of us are afraid of pain and injury.

When I was first trying to learn the basic swing and force out, I developed a chronic cycle of fear due to my repeated failure. The swing looks simple enough but is, in fact, very difficult. To build a good swing, the flyer must throw his body backward and forward in a pendular motion in a rhythm that complements and extends the natural arc of the trapeze. If the timing of any of his kicks is not right, it will kill the swing and might cause him to approach the board on the backswing at the wrong angle and whack his legs. For two or three months, the intricate moves eluded me. I didn't have the necessary strength, flexibility, or the timing. Consequently, almost every time I attempted a vigorous swing I hit my legs or buttocks on the pedestal board on the return swing. Two or three times each session a dull thud would resound through the area—the sound of one cheek clapping, of a leg or two meeting solid wood. Within the hour a delicate blue bruise line would appear somewhere on my rear anatomy.

Not surprisingly, I began to develop a minor phobia—a fear of crashing. Climbing to the platform, I would visualize each movement, pump up my willpower, and launch myself into the pendulum. But a vicious feedback loop contaminated my consciousness. The cellular memory of pain tightened my muscles and increased my determination to get it right. Then my exaggerated effort produced the exact result I was trying to avoid—thud. Another bruise. Each night my wife, Jan, who was by now an expert on abrasions and contusions, would examine me, apply unguents, and offer running commentary: "Oh, that is a pretty one. Tonight's red scrape goes nicely with last week's purple, which is beginning to blend into yellow. Your rear end looks like a vivid sunset, a smoggy night in Los Angeles, or like you got a caning in Singapore for misconduct."

One afternoon my teacher was shouting the same old instructions to me from the ground, "Kick back, legs forward, force out, kick back harder, pike . . .'' as I crashed repeatedly into the pedestal. In my frustration I thought of the old adage ''If things don't get better soon, I may have to ask you to stop helping me'' and determined to ignore all advice and try something new. Perhaps, if I shut my eyes I might be able to *feel* the movement rather than trying to perfect the moves that I had *imagined* and failed to execute a hundred times. I made several false starts before I screwed up my courage to swing blind. Finally, I shut my eyes, lifted the bar over my head, kept my arms straight, stepped off into the void, and entered the arc— and this time, something rare happened. My hips began to sway and make love to the pendulum inscribed by the trapeze. Out I swung, snake-hipped, kicked up at the apex, and glided downward until I whipped back and rose above the pedestal, my body in a perfect 7. No thud. Two more swings. Still no thud.

For a long time I savored the kinesthetic memory of the lithe movements and the sigh of relief from my long-suffering southern extremities. Then, I went back up to try it again, faithful to the advice of the great fictional guru of flyers and catchers—Burt Lancaster, alias Mike Ribble—who speaks to us from the film *Trapeze*, ''Now that he has it, don't let him lose it.'' With my eyes alternately shut and open, I practiced again and again, each swing getting more fluid, until my shoulders begged for rest and I knew I had broken the cycle of dread.

Each time I triumph over a minor fear, I get a shot of pure vitality straight into the center of my being. For several days after I lost my fear of smashing into the board, I felt a quiet joy in my loins, not unlike the afterglow that remains after lovemaking. There was a new imprint, a bit of carnal knowledge, a muscular memory lodged in my viscera. This new knowledge was not mental, and it did not reside in my imagination. I still could not visualize what I had learned but I could feel it in my midsection. It was a form of tacit knowledge, blind but powerful, a body wisdom my mind could not fully comprehend. Now the tyranny of the negative feedback loop was broken, the energy that had been tied up in fear was liberated and I could get way more into the swing of things.

The practice of trapeze provides me with a daily occasion to become a connoisseur of my fears, to see where they reside in my body and to separate the rational from the irrational. This discipline is similar to the science of fear—*phobologia*—the ancient Spartans used to train soldiers to be fearless in battle (as imagined by Steven Pressfield in his novel *Gates of Fire,* Doubleday Books, NY, 1998) Fear, the Spartans observed, accumulates in specific sites in the body—in the muscles of the jaw, neck, and eyes, in the shoulder girdles, the lungs and heart, hands and knees, loins and back. Therefore, they reasoned, if the tensed muscles in these sites can be relaxed, the cycle of fear that leads to panic can be interrupted. To accomplish this, they developed a series of exercises that creates an exquisite awareness of the muscular holding patterns in various parts of the body that accompany fear. Once aware of the muscular tension, the master of phobologia can relax the mind and become fearless—aphobic—in the presence of danger.

When I stand on the pedestal poised to throw a trick, I pause and take an inventory of my body—eyes squinting, hands sweating, chest narrowing, knees trembling, stomach jittering, mind filling with catastrophic images. Then, I breathe deeply and invite my muscles to release their burden of fear. When I neither force myself to be fearless nor run away from the danger, an area of freedom opens up within which I discover new options. I cease to be a victim of my fear and I break the hypnotic cycle of dread, the vicious feedback loop, the self-fulfilling prophecy of failure that shrinks my world.

A fear a day keeps the psychiatrist away. Fear is an inevitable part of the human condition. Because we are all flying through time toward oblivion, we grasp and hold too tight, squeeze the life out of life. We conspire to avoid awareness of our primal fear, our anxiety about existence, by cultivating the illusion that we are exceptional, invulnerable, immortal, immune to the perils, sufferings, and tragedies that afflict lesser human beings. Our denial of death causes us to become deluded, grandiose, neurotic, disembodied, and unreal. Albert Camus once said that it was only after we accept the absurdity of the world that we can begin to write a manual of happiness. Paradoxically, when we invite our fears into the hearth of our awareness, they cease to be an undifferentiated mass of terrifying demons and become tolerable guests. Each day befriend a single fear and the miscellaneous terrors of being human will never join together to form such a morass of vague anxiety that it rules your life from the shadows of the unconscious. We learn to fly not by becoming fearless, but by the daily practice of courage.

What is the appeal of danger? Why take risks and live with unnecessary fears? Isn't this masochistic?

As I learn to control the flood tide of adrenaline, I notice there is something highly erotic about living in a conscious relationship to danger and fear. Each time I work on a trick that is near the edge of my capacity, I taste that intoxicating mixture of fear and excitement, dread and pleasure, that sustains bullfighters, mountain climbers, deep-sea divers, race-car drivers, and trapeze artists.

My friend Jim Peterson, a senior editor of *Playboy,* test-drives new motorcycles at high speeds. "Adrenaline is God's own aphrodisiac," he says. One classic psychological study had one group of men cross a narrow swinging bridge over a gorge and another group cross a solid, secure bridge. Each group was met by an attractive female researcher and was later asked if they would like to date her. Eight out of ten who crossed the dangerous bridge and two out of ten who crossed the secure bridge said they would like to date her. Ever since Hemingway exposed and celebrated the link between bullfighting and sexual passion, there has been a suspicion abroad that thrill seekers are slightly perverse folk who need danger either as a sexual stimulant or as a substitute for sex.

Adrenaline may make the heart grow fonder, but there are more profound reasons for courting danger. The presence of danger makes us feel intensely alive.

Many years ago I was camping on a small beach on the French Riviera that was surrounded by high cliffs. When I reached my tolerance level for sunbathing and lying about, I decided to climb the cliff. For the first one hundred feet the rock was solid and offered good hand- and footholds, and I made rapid progress. But gradually the rock became soft and loose, and I was not aware of it until I reached for a hold on an overhang and a fifty-pound chunk directly above me teetered when I touched it. That way blocked, I looked for an alternate route and was startled to realize that the entire upper section of the cliff was unstable. As I turned to retrace my steps I had the sickening realization that my retreat was also blocked by unstable rock. Through inattention and stupidity, I had maneuvered myself into a position from which I could not move without extreme danger. My legs began to shake and my fear quickly escalated into full-blown panic. I realized that I had to calm myself or I would fall, so I forced myself to breathe slowly. When my panic abated, I noticed a possible route across the face of the rock to a chimney that led to the top of the cliff. Slowly and carefully, I traversed the rock, testing its stability before I took each step. I don't know how long it took me to reach the chimney, but when I got there I climbed the remaining fifty feet to freedom in no time at all.

Safely on top, I began to run along a narrow path through

thickets, whooping and hollering at the top of my lungs. The acuity of each of my senses became supernormal. I felt the briars cutting my legs but the pain was immediately translated into an exquisite sensation of joy at being alive. Small flowers, each one etched clearly against the background of grass, exploded into my vision. Birdsongs, amplified a hundred times, blasted their way out of the afternoon silence into my ears. The scent of violets rolled into my nostrils in great waves. The peanut butter, honey, and bread I ate when I reached camp a half-hour later were ambrosial. For nearly a week I remained in this state of psychedelic awareness, awash in a sense of wonder and gratitude for being alive.

For me, living with the danger of flying is becoming a kind of daily prayer or meditation practice. The discipline I have adopted for myself is this. Each day I choose some trick or move that is in the range of my ability but which still frightens me, and I practice it several times as an exercise in keeping my dialogue with fear conscious. Facing danger allows me to make an inventory of my fears, gives me an index of my courage, and forces me to develop grace under pressure.

As nearly as I can figure, the rock-bottom truth is that life is both wonderful and terrifying. The German philosopher Rudolf Otto said that our confrontation with that ultimate reality within which we live and move and have our being (which, for lack of a better name, we call the Holy) is always a mystery that evokes both fascination and fear. This infinitely precious gift of life may be taken from any of us at any moment by accident, disease, or tragedy. At best, the human condition offers us a grave joy.

This suggests that to ask "Why face danger?" is the wrong question. The right question is "What happens if I try to build a life dedicated to avoiding all danger and all unnecessary risk?"

47

If "security" and "safety" become watchwords by which I live, gradually the circle of my experience becomes small and claustrophobic.

I need to live near the vital edge between fear and fascination to help me remember that, so long as I live, I will tremble and wonder.

Of course, it is possible to become addicted to thrills, chills, and spills. You can tell if you are an excitement junky when any single activity becomes the sole focus of your sense of aliveness and excitement. When risk-taking becomes the only antidote for boredom, it is a dangerous drug. A friend of mine who is a doctor and an amateur flyer told me, "Trapeze is the only exciting thing in my life. Without it my life would be boring and meaningless." I worry about him. I wonder why he is not excited about his marriage, his children, his community, his vocation. Addiction is monofocal and destructive no matter whether the drug is alcohol, work, or golf. Vitality is polyfocal. I joke about being addicted to trapeze, but in truth my life is rich in satisfactions: my family, friends, farm, and work all give me daily pleasure and a sense of worthiness.

The right use of danger is to increase our overall sense of the wonder and worth of our ordinary moments, activities, and relationships.

There is an important distinction between being foolhardy and spirited in playing near the brink of danger.

When I was a graduate student I had the rare good fortune to spend an afternoon with Gabriel Marcel, the French philosopher about whose work I wrote my doctoral dissertation. As I was dodging through the traffic in Harvard Square, my wife Heather said to him, "Sam likes to take risks."

Marcel replied, with a twinkle in his eye, "Only take interesting risks."

Each of us must decide what risks are acceptable for us. I

know of at least one highly accomplished flyer, Lisa Hofsess, who began her flying career at the YMCA in Denver, became a professional flyer, and later stopped flying.

"Why?" I asked her.

"A lot of trapeze enthusiasts live with a high degree of denial and refuse to be aware of the real danger involved," she said. "One of my friends was doing a one-and-a-half somersault to a legs catch, missed, fell into the net, and was paralyzed. After that, I realized that for me flying was an unacceptable risk."

These days, all of us in the San Francisco trapeze community live with an acute sense of danger as we have been saddened and sobered by the recent death of a lovely young woman—a highly accomplished single-swinging-trapeze performer—who, unaccountably, neglected to fasten her safety belt and fell to her death. She has become our silent companion and, because of her, we fly with greater caution and a poignant sense of our own mortality.

I follow the basic maxim of trapeze work: avoid unnecessary risks. Never push yourself to do something that is beyond your level of competence. During the first months of my training, I was confined to the safety lines that allow novice flyers to practice swinging, falling to the net, going to the catcher, and simple tricks with a minimum of risk. Intellectually, I understood that my risk was small because the man on the safety lines could stop my fall before I hit the net at a dangerous angle. I suffered from skinned knees and elbows and net burns on my prominent nose but no broken bones.

But flying with lines is like making love with a condom; it is safer but not so free. Inevitably, the time came when I longed for the freedom of flying without a safety belt. Repeatedly, I asked myself, "Am I ready to solo?"

Nevertheless, it came as a shock when my teacher announced, "Sam, I think you're ready to fall to the net without lines. Your swing is adequate and you have a pretty good sense of your body position. So, here is what you do. Take off from the board and let your swing die down a little. Then, wait until you are at the static point at the end of the swing, release the bar, lift your legs, and drop to the net. You need to decide before you let go of the bar whether you want to drop to your seat or your back. If you go for the seat drop, keep your body in an L shape with your legs extended and your arms at your side. If you go for the back drop, land flat with your arms extended. What you want to avoid is hitting the net with your body in a V, because that will cause you to whiplash and slam your face into your knees. Any questions?"

I had studied the net drop for long enough to understand what I needed to do and was intellectually convinced I was ready for it. Nevertheless, my hands began to sweat and my stomach turned flips as I climbed onto the pedestal. I grasped the bar so tightly I probably left my fingerprints on the tape, and took off. Back and forth I swung through several arcs of the pendulum as I had done a hundred times, but this time everything was different. I seemed to be over an abyss rather than a net. And I was all alone. I think my teacher was shouting something to me but I couldn't hear what he was saying. For a fleeting instant I had the illusion that I could cancel the whole experiment by yelling, "I changed my mind. I'm not ready. Hold me on the safety lines." Then, reality struck. There would be no rescue. It was either the seat drop or the back drop, and I was on my own. I decided for the seat, released the fly bar, and fell for a long time before I landed in the net halfway between the L and the V, bounced like a crooked ball, and came to rest. I made a quick inventory of my body parts, found them all in working order, let out a victory whoop, and descended from the net with an exhalation of meadowlarks singing in the vast, new space of freedom that had opened up within my chest.

Death says, "Play it safe." Life says, "Risk it." At the vital edge something dangerous calls my name. What will I risk to stay alive?

CHAPTER 4

The Leap of Faith

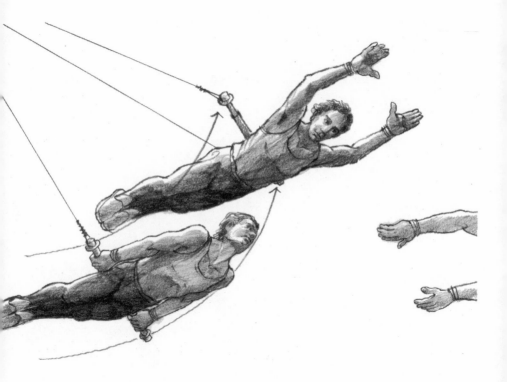

Without risk there is no faith, and the greater
the risk, the greater the faith.

Søren Kierkegaard

Outside the window of my studio, a summer
warbler has built her nest and is raising her brood. After days of
her stuffing their waiting beaks with a thousand insects, the
moment has arrived for the great launching. Today flying lessons begin. Mom brings a tasty morsel from the deli, but
instead of serving it up, she perches out of reach to coax the
little squeakers to the edge of the nest. The boldest of the
bunch stretches its neck out over the abyss hoping for a bit of
breakfast but loses its balance and flaps its wings awkwardly.
Mom rewards the effort and goes hunting for more juicy bits.
For hours the inducements continue until one reluctant
fledgling leans too far, loses its balance, falls, flaps its wings,
and flies to the nearest branch. Being myself something of a
fledgling, I imagine that my fellow flyer feels both flabbergasted
and triumphant.

Flying begins with a leap of faith.

For the novice, there is a lot of flapping of wings before the
first solo flight. Even before the basic skills of swinging and
dropping to the net have been mastered, a flexible fledgling can
accomplish a knee-hang catch. Since this first trip to the catcher
involves no air time it requires a minimum of trust. The flyer
leaves the board, brings her legs up and over the bar, and drops

into a knee hang on the first swing. At the point where the flyer's and catcher's arcs intersect, the catcher grasps the flyer's wrists, yells, "I've got you," and only then does the flyer release her knees from the bar.

The real leap of faith comes when the flyer attempts the first release trick—a bird's nest, plange, or splits. Arched beneath the bar in one of these positions—like an oriole's nest hung in the fork of a tree, a banana curved around a stick, or a dancer doing the splits—the flyer swings out to the highest point of the pendulum, waits until the catcher shouts, "Hep," releases the trapeze, and flies.

The gap between two pairs of outstretched arms is only a few feet that could be traversed in a millisecond. But between the "Hep" and the catch there is a journey across an abyss. No footbridge leads from reason to faith, from doubt to trust. Prior to the leap, fear seems more justified than trust, isolation more fundamental than communion, and the flight of the spirit an impossibility.

The short leap from the trapeze to the catcher is a flight from primal fear to basic trust, from I to thou, from autonomy to communion, that can only be made by a total commitment of the self. Flying, like faith, hope, and love, is an existential act that cannot be accomplished by a spectator. Without the mutual trust and action of flyer and catcher, there is no trick, no art, no transcendence of individuality and isolation.

When I had mastered the preliminary skills and done a dozen or more knee-hang catches, I began practicing the three easy positions. After a couple of weeks, I concluded that the bird's nest required more flexibility in my back and the splits more stretch in my crotch than was comfortable, so I settled on the plange for my first flight. I had plenty of strength to hold myself curved beneath the bar, and the position felt more elegant than the others.

In the fullness of time, on one ordinary Wednesday evening, the moment arrived for my metamorphosis from pedestrian to flyer. After the usual period of warm-up and practice, the catcher climbed to his perch and I to the pedestal. He swung high, went into his lock. I took off well, pulled my legs up, threaded them through my arms, locked my body into the curved plange position, and swung out to meet him. As we reached the point of intersection, he shouted "Hep" and . . . Nothing. My hands simply refused to obey the command of my mind. Far from releasing, they grasped the bar with a death grip. I swung back, reversing all of my moves, and dropped to the net—disappointed.

"You were in perfect position and the timing was right. What happened?" my teacher asked.

"I don't know," I answered. "I just froze. I couldn't let go."

"Let's try it again. Do everything the same way. But let go this time."

Second attempt—same story. Third attempt—same story. The evening ended without my having earned my wings.

When I got home and had my ritual bath and brandy, simmering in my disappointment, I began to ponder the reasons for my extraordinary tenacity in refusing to make my inaugural flight. Why was I so reluctant to make the leap of faith? Was this refusal to fly only a momentary timidity or did it reflect something deeper in my character?

The first thing that popped into mind during my midnight meditation was an incident that had happened a couple of weeks before. Rebecca Perez, a single-swinging-trapeze artist, had just returned from a tour with a circus and had set up her trapeze at the San Francisco School so she could work on her routine during her off-season. We all watched as she performed a dizzying array of standing hop offs, twisting ankle catches, and toe hangs with perfect ease while swinging in a 180-degree pendulum arc. One day she was persuaded to try the flying trapeze.

To everyone's amazement she was as fearful as any amateur and refused to go to the catcher.

"No way," she said. "On the single swinging trapeze I'm in control. It's all me. I trust myself and know my own strengths and limitations but I don't have to depend on anyone else."

Her observation about herself struck home with me. I don't trust easily nor am I eager to surrender control.

There are good reasons for this. I once took the great leap of faith—and fell hard. I was brought up within the bosom of Protestant fundamentalism, and by the time I was eleven years old I had placed all the faith I could muster in the miracle, mystery, and authority of the Bible, the Presbyterian church, and the theology of John Calvin. When I went to Harvard Divinity School and began serious study of the Bible, church history, and comparative religions, I discovered that the "Fundamental Truths" I had been taught were false—"they ain't necessarily so."

In reaction to the disillusionment and spiritual confusion caused by my overbelief, I determined that I would pursue a path of reason and never again make the mistake of placing blind faith in any authority, ideology, or institution. As all recovering fundamentalists know—whether Christian, Marxist, or Freudian—once faith has been misplaced it is hard to recover. And the memory of paradise lost is long. As Howard Thurman said, "Nothing binds us so tightly as the chains we have broken."

As a philosopher, I am committed to questioning and entertaining doubts about all orthodoxies, ideologies, and belief systems whether theological, political, economic, or psychological. I refuse to place absolute faith in Jesus, Progress, the market economy, psychotherapy, Guru XYZ, or any of the Grand Inquisitors who promise peace of mind.

With regard to God—with all His-Her-Its-Their aliases—I

remain agnostic but hopeful. To take the leap of faith is to commit oneself to live by the maxim "In God we trust." But what if there is no God, no Ultimate Catcher, no everlasting arms? If I am to risk the abyss, I would like reasonable assurances that I will be caught.

My meditations also brought to mind other painful experiences of leaping and falling—in love. Like most romantics, I have (more than once) pledged my undying love to some incarnate goddess. With passionate abandon I leaped into the arms of my One True Love only to find that She had abandoned me for another. (In fairness, I must confess I was as often the abandoner as the abandoned; I have also dropped a couple or three consorts who risked the flight to my arms.) After I crashed, recovered, leaped, crashed, recovered, leaped a few times, I vowed that I would never again *fall* in love. *Grow* in love? Perhaps. But let it be gradual, pedestrian, step-by-step.

My midnight reflections reassured me that my caution, my refusal to leap into blind faith or blind love, was reasonable and right. Maybe I should give up the dream of flying trapeze and take up the single trapeze where I would never have to fly to the hands of the catcher. This way I could depend on the strength of my own arms to rock 'n' roll and swing 'n' sway but never have to risk flying united. Solitude may be lonely, but it is safe.

Just when I was getting comfortable with this notion and preparing myself to accept a pedestrian existence, my mind threw a twisting somersault and presented me with a paradox, a dilemma, a koan. It is reasonable to play it safe, not to leap—but it is not reasonable always to be reasonable. As Blaise Pascal said, "The heart has reasons the mind knows not of." There is no way to enjoy the comfort of faith or the ecstasy of love without making a wholehearted, existential commitment of the self. Faith, love, and flying all depend on a relationship that can be created only by an act of trust that involves taking the risk of falling into the void. Before the fact, all risks are folly. It is only after a successful flight to the arms of the catcher that the risky decision to trust is seen as the essence of wisdom.

By the time Wednesday rolled around again, I understood that the decision I had to make was not about throwing a trick, but about my character, my willingness to move beyond solo to soul.

I was strangely calm when my turn came. I won't say that I was without fear, but somewhere beneath, beyond, or above the dominion of my mind I had already made the leap. I had decided that I would take the leap again. And again, and again. This time when I heard my name called and the "Hep" sounded, I released the bar, surrendered to the void, and fell to the hands of the catcher.

CHAPTER 5

Creating a Graceful Body

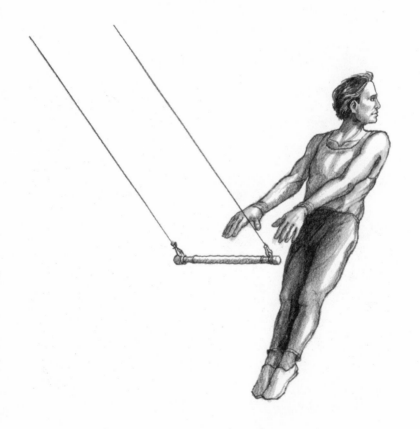

*The art of the flying trapeze emerged within the Romanticism of the
nineteenth century. . . . To the Romantics, aerial performers seemed the
personification of the glorified body, the great explorers of the outer range
of the human potential.*

Steve Gossard in *A Reckless Era of Aerial Performance*

My leap of faith led to a serious commitment.
If I was to progress as a flyer, I would have to find some way to
practice more frequently than the two evenings a week I was
traveling to the San Francisco School of Circus Arts.

By now it was winter, the rainy season in California, and
every time I attempted to swing on my makeshift outdoor trapeze in the tree, a fresh shower cascaded down on my head. It
became obvious to me—and, with a little persuasion, to my
long-suffering wife—that the only reasonable solution was to
hang a small trapeze in our dining room so I could practice in
foul weather or fair. Fortunately, when I built my house I made
a massive living room (thirty-two by thirty-two with sixteen-
foot ceilings), innocent of any premonition that it would be a
perfect place for a swinging trapeze. A little work with drills
and augers, a few industrial-strength screw eyes, and I installed
a padded practice trapeze with eight-foot cables.

Of course, every solution breeds a new problem. With my
daily discipline I grew muscles in places I previously did not
know even existed. Supernatural bumps appeared in my arms,
back, and shoulders, and my skin began to feel stretched. I
definitely pumped up, but my strenuous practice began to take
a toll on my body.

For openers, I was well into the decade when senior citizens are offered discounts at movies, the AARP advises retirement, and catalogues arrive in the mail featuring products to deal with adult incontinence. Although I had always enjoyed good health and was in reasonably good physical condition, I was, as they say, "chronologically challenged." If I multiplied 62 by 178 by 74 inches (age by weight by height), the sum was in excess of any reasonable maximum for a flyer.

Age aside, I am still not constructed to be a flyer.

Small flyers, male or female, have an advantage in that their bodies are usually more symmetrical and their movements quicker than those of fat, tall, or rangy folk. And it is obviously easier to catch a light bundle hurtling through the air than a heavy one. An ideal flyer is light and lithe, a sprite, with sinuous arms and abs of steel. Of the great flyers of the last generation, Tony Steele was a short 5 feet 4 inches, Reggie Armor was 5 feet 7 inches, Fay Alexander was 5 feet 9 inches. Tito Gaona, the most flamboyant flyer of the 1980s, is the ideal height and weight—5 feet 6 inches and 155 pounds. Miguel Vazquez is of such a slight build—5 feet 7 inches and 137 pounds—that at a quick glance you might mistake him for a librarian. His arms seem almost frail, his chest is no broader than average, his skin is delicate and nearly transparent. Only the upright thrust of his posture and the way he seems to glide as he walks suggest anything out of the ordinary. He exhibits no bulging muscles, no bravado or machismo.

As Plato observed, the real usually deviates from the ideal. Actual flyers come in all shapes and sizes. In what must have been one of the most unusual acts of the 1920s, the Flying Melzoras consisted of Ray Melzer, who was known for spinning the artificial foot at the end of his artificial leg as he swung from the pedestal board, his brother Buster, who weighed over 230 pounds, and their mother—"Ma"—who worked as the catcher for the troupe into her sixties. Ray Valentine Jr., the fifth generation of Flying Valentines, was a slender lad of nine when he became the youngest flyer in history to perform a triple somersault. But he grew to be 6 feet and 225 pounds. Currently, he is too heavy for most catchers, so he throws the triple to a trapeze that is attached by arm-length cables from the catcher's trapeze and placed in his hands by the catcher as he comes out of his final somersault.

It is generally reckoned that a flyer has between twelve and fifteen years to practice his art. Shoulder injuries are the occupational hazard that force most to retire before they reach forty. At sixty-two my shoulders were ancient, but virginal, underdeveloped but not overstressed. When I began to practice daily, however, a cacophony of minor pains began to accompany my vigorous pleasures. There were throbbing pulsations from complaining tendons of arms and shoulders, spiraling whines of a twisted back, staccato stabs of open blisters that hardened into calluses, and rasping irritations from net burns. Like an aging husband married to an athletic young bride, my body was not prepared to cope with the desires of my spirit.

My aches and pains announced that I was going to have to develop a new relationship with my body. I needed a measure of physical re-creation that was just short of a resurrection of the body. I knew what the poet Wislawa Szymborska meant when she spoke about the trapeze artist who has to weave his way through his own former shape and work "to seize this swaying world/by stretching out the arms he has conceived." Like him I would have to remake my body to do the bidding of my spirit.

First came the arms and shoulders. As the tendinitis and unidentified pains around my rotator cuffs spread downward and joined forces with the legions of their kindred advancing upward from the elbows, I sought relief from the standard unguents and medications—Aspirin and Tiger Balm. My physician suggested I take up a gentlemanly sport like golf, or ice my injuries and rest a lot. Following each practice session in the city, I carried my rubber ice bags into the nearest McDonald's and asked the clerk to fill them, whereupon I cinched both around my overheated arms and drove home looking like a man with a severe case of elephantitis.

A couple of stubborn pockets of tendinitis would not yield to any nostrum, so I decided to try my local sports-injury therapist. Once he had me on his table, he put his fingers delicately on the most inflamed spots on my shoulders and began to twang back and forth on my tendons like an eight-hundred-pound gorilla playing a twelve-string guitar. As he plucked away mercilessly, he explained that tendons have very little blood supply and so must be rigorously stimulated. Periodically, the pain from his "rigorous stimulation" got so severe I had to ask him to stop and allow me to get my breath. Normally, I seek pleasure and try to avoid pain, so at the end of the session I resolved not to seek any more painful cures for pain. The next day, however, the tendinitis was gone and my arms felt as if they had been restructured, lubricated, and lengthened. Subsequently, he taught me how to torture my own tendons for the sake of my art.

My next lesson had to do with the need to balance strength with strength. As the result of swinging from the trapeze, the muscles of my forearms needed for grasping and holding became abnormally developed and chronically tense. Strengthen a muscle and you shorten it, which has the effect of lengthening the antagonist muscle and creating an imbalance. Develop any potential and you tend to neglect its opposite. Overdevelopment is the Siamese twin of underdevelopment. (Thus the world cannot forever exist half-rich and half-poor.) The Greeks understood this and made an ideal of *sophrosyne*—harmony or balance. The ability to grasp and hold firmly needs to be balanced by the ability to release and stretch.

With a little experimentation, I found I could balance the muscles of my forearms by wrapping rubber bands—the ones that hold bunches of broccoli together were the perfect size and strength—around my fingers and forcing my hand to open. For a time I worked with Nautilus machines at the local health club to develop arms and back muscles that were underused in trapeze, but I abandoned the project because of my low tolerance for boredom. Ten minutes of intimacy with a machine feels like a long, bad marriage.

Then there was the matter of stretching. Rigidity is an article of faith for the American male. Our heroes stand tall, alone, and unbending. Compare Clint Eastwood to Bruce Lee and you will see what I mean. The Eastern ideal—as exemplified in the martial arts, meditation, and yoga—makes flexibility a defining virtue of the Way. The reed that bends in the wind does not break. "Yield and overcome. Bend and be straight. Empty and be full," the *Tao Te Ching* advises. In any park in San Francisco, of an early morning, you can see ancient (older than I) Chinese men and women practicing the fluid motions of tai chi chuan. As an heir to the rigidities of both the American and the Presbyterian mythologies, I had added new muscle to old muscle and increased my strength but diminished my range of motion. I needed to be less upstanding, less stiff.

At first, stretching seemed both painful and a waste of time. Let's quit warming up and get on with the action! But soon it became a way of life. Cross-leg stretches and back rolls before I got out of bed. Pass no doorway without pushing against the frame to widen and stretch the shoulders. Jump to the trapeze bar in the living room and hang out a bit before breakfast. Touch those toes morning, noon, and night, especially before getting on jet planes. After a year, an objective observer would still not describe me as lithe, limber, or agile but I was more flexible than I had been as a young man, which isn't saying much. But when I hear my teacher say, "Keep your legs straight and kick back hard, open your chest and arch your back as if your body was a bow," I no longer despair of my rigidity. I am learning the way of a reed in the wind.

There are moments when the trapeze rig feels like a medieval rack, a torture device. It exacts a measure of pain but it does add a cubit to your stature. In the beginning, hanging on the bar stretches and strains muscles that have been used scarcely at all since the naked ape came down from the trees and adopted the upright posture. The hands redden and blister for months in spite of tape, gauze, grips, and chalk. Then, gradually, three lines of callouses begin to replace blisters to form a kind of pocket within which the fly bar fits. Husbands, wives, and lovers of flyers complain, "When you touch me it feels like some animal is rubbing its hooves over my skin." In secret, initiates cherish and compare their wounds. Blisters and callouses, like dueling scars, tattoos, or body piercing, become perverse adornments, beauty marks appreciated only by other members of the cult. The minor pain, like a love bite, is blended into the ecstatic moments of flight and transmuted into erotic pleasure.

In addition to minor pains there were injuries to contend with—pulled and torn muscles, a twisted back, and net burns. Once I cracked a rib or two and was forced to abstain from flying for six weeks, an abstinence I did not suffer gracefully, according to my wife, who alleged that I was more worried about missing a few weeks of trapeze than I was of killing myself. In truth, the risk of cracked ribs seems to me the price of remaining physically vigorous in the second half of life. Otherwise, I am tempted to become sedentary. Instead of running down a moderate embankment I become timid and edge down sideways. The fear of falling because one is no longer agile easily becomes a self-fulfilling prophesy. We get old because we stop playing, not vice versa.

As my body makeover progressed, my muscles lengthened, grew stronger and more balanced, and the time came when I could practice daily without lingering discomfort. But as these changes in my physical body took place, I began to realize that I faced a far more subtle challenge, which I can best characterize as the need to transform my spiritual body or my imaginal body.

To explain what I mean I need to invoke one of my philosophical mentors from an earlier era of my life. In the hip 1960s, I was much influenced by philosopher Norman O. Brown's radical revision of Freud in *Love's Body*. "The reality of the body is not given, but is to be built not with hands but by the spirit. It is the poetic body." This notion excited me because it suggested that the body we are given at birth is not a finished biological entity; it is a potentiality waiting to be informed by our intentions, our wills, our dreams. We are *bio-mythic animals*. The true double helix that makes us human is an intertwining of biological mechanisms (or DNA) and cultural mechanisms (or myths). We are fabric woven of chemistry and narrative, biology and stories, flesh and dreams.

When I became convinced that my body was, literally, informed by a myth, a dream, a story, I realized I could discover what underlying self-image was unconsciously programming me by making a careful analysis of my physical body. The habitual way in which our muscles and tendons create a dynamic structure, in sickness or in health (what psychologist Wilhelm Reich called our "character-armor"), provides us with a topographical map of our psyches. Our physical bodies are palimpsests—ancient parchments on which our cultures have written their stories, myths, and values, but the memory of this process has been repressed. It is the nature of the myths that program our perceptions of self and world to remain largely unconscious, because every culture claims its dominant mythology is "the truth," the one accurate account of reality. We internalize our cultural and family myths by a process of social osmosis that begins when we are infants; therefore, the process by which we arrive at our view of self and world is erased from awareness. If, however, we pay close attention to the story that is inscribed on our body, we can discern "beneath" it the outlines of the graceful body—our original face, our essence.

The story that has in-formed my body for most of my life is not difficult to decipher. It began in ninth grade on the day I lost a fistfight and was embarrassed by the frailty, timidity, and weakness of my body. While the cuts were still festering from where my enemy had rubbed my face in the gravel, I sent away for a Charles Atlas course in bodybuilding, determined never to be a humiliated ninety-eight-pound weakling. For the next two decades I wrestled competitively, practiced bodybuilding, and developed the ideal small waist, washboard stomach, and expanded chest.

It was not until I began to suffer from what is variously called an identity crisis or a midlife transition that it occurred to me I had constructed a warrior's body. My chronically tightened stomach (so unlike the Buddha) and puffed-out chest were a form of psychological armor. My battle-hardened body was designed for combat against an enemy. I was well defended against the softer emotions, better at anger than grief, better at conquest than surrender, better at work than play, better at control than wonder. I was strong but unbending. In short, a good American man—an antagonist, competitor, warrior.

Now that I have strengthened my muscles and tendons enough to do my bidding, the great challenge is to transform my myth-body, my dream-body, my spirit-body. I must leave behind the body-psyche of the warrior, weave my way through my own former shape, and exchange a battle-hardened body for an airborne body.

Thus far, I have been a man of gravity—serious, strong, rigid, taut, heavy, and earthbound. It is time for levity, lightness, litheness, and soaring.

CHAPTER 6

The Discipline of Beauty

We have no art.
We do everything as beautifully as possible.

Balinese proverb

An important *clue* about how to create a lighter-than-air spirit-body came to me when I was mulling over a phrase I had heard a hundred times but had never taken to heart.

One of the earliest sets of instructions a novice flyer hears is "smile and point your toes." At first I thought it was just a kind of wise-ass refrain the teacher used to distract fledglings from their fear, but as I thought more about it, I realized that this miniliturgy is not meant as an instruction for cosmetic beauty or pleasing the audience. Looking good on the trapeze is a matter not of vanity but of necessity. If the movement isn't graceful, it isn't right. Beauty is not optional.

Trapeze is *not* primarily about defying death, courting danger, or taking risks. It is about creating beauty. Once, one of our best flyers was just about to throw a double somersault. The catcher yelled over to him, "Let's do it right and make some beauty."

If, as Henry James said, "in art economy is always beauty," the essence of the art of the trapeze is economy of form and movement. Arms and legs must not dangle but must be tucked into a streamlined aerodynamic form. The great philosophical principle of Ockham's Razor that defines the nature of scientific explanations—"Entities must not be unnecessarily multiplied"—applies equally to the aerial arts. Any extraneous movement destroys the rhythm. Form follows function. Either you do it beautifully or you do it wrong.

When I watch films of Alfredo Cadona, it is easy to see why he remains the template against which contemporary flyers still measure themselves. His every move is pure animal grace. He is a snake gliding through the grass, a cat turning in midair, a cheetah in pursuit. He is Picasso painting on a canvas of pure space using a minimum of strokes. He is a master of the art of subtracting the superfluous. Art Concello, the flyer who replaced Cadona in Ringling Brothers after he was injured, said of him, "If Alfredo had been run over by a truck, he'd have done it so gracefully that your first instinct might have been to applaud."

Perfection in art does not lead to perfection in life, however. Although Cadona was the essence of aerial grace, in love he was a tragic figure. At the height of his career he married Lillian Leitzel, the most famous aerialist of her day. But the reign of the King and Queen of Trapeze was brief. In 1931 she fell to her death on the arena floor when her rigging broke. When she died, Alfredo became reckless and, in rebound from his grief, married Vera Bruce, a member of his troupe. When she divorced him and tried to take possession of all of Leitzel's personal effects, he arranged a meeting in their lawyer's office, shot her fatally and turned the gun on himself. The art of living involves a kind of moral elegance, which requires that we give the same commitment, attention, and creative eros to our interpersonal relationships as we would give to painting, music, or dance.

My early effort to learn the intricate movements of the basic swing and force out became an important part of my artistic education. One day I was huffing and puffing and expending a lot of energy because my legs were swinging at cross-purpose to the momentum of the rest of my body, and I got the bright idea of placing a dollar bill between my ankles and trying to swing without dropping it. My takeoff was awkward but the experiment was an immediate success. The dollar remained in place throughout my swing and dismount to the net. For the first time my body was in one piece, because this simple device forced me to keep my legs together and my toes pointed, which in turn forced me to initiate all my movements from my center, which made my swing simple, supple, and beautiful.

After this minor triumph I continued, repeatedly, working on returning from the catcher to the trapeze, a move in which I habitually have trouble getting into the right position to make the leap. My teacher gave me an elaborate set of instructions: "Do more of everything. Take off higher, force out stronger, so you will be higher when you reach the catch point. When you are swinging with the catcher, force out in the apron, ride downhill, then sweep back hard, bring your body into a 7, push against his hands, turn and reach for the trapeze."

Dutifully, I climbed to the pedestal, doubled my effort, and tried several times to follow his instructions. But the more I tried to change everything at once, the more chaotic my movements became. My midair dance resembled nothing so much as a frog on amphetamines.

Happily, one of the Flying Gaonas, Richie Gaona, a Hollywood stuntman and master teacher to Los Angeles fledgling flyers, happened to be visiting that day and overheard the instructions. He sidled over to me and gave me a suggestion. "Forget all that for the moment. Just try to kick the catcher when you make your turn to catch the trapeze and that will automatically put your legs in the right position." I tried it and it worked. As in most arts, less is more.

When I was younger and filled with utopian dreams of remaking myself and the world into something resembling perfection, I periodically instituted sweeping reforms. I would decide, on blue Monday, that I had to change everything about my life. I would begin a three-day fast, start an intensive exercise program, quit smoking, stop eating sugar, begin to meditate, read only edifying books, immerse myself in programs for political and social change. Predictably enough, my utopian schemes—like those of Joseph Stalin or Pol Pot—would then collapse and leave despair in their wake. If I couldn't change *everything* what was the sense of trying to change *anything?*

Gradually, I came to appreciate the principle of minimum interference. Sometimes, when I am feeling impotent to alleviate the burden of human suffering, it is enough to look directly into the eyes of a homeless person and smile. Sometimes, all I need to do to lift myself out of the Slough of Despond is to sit quietly and breathe deeply. Sometimes, I can resolve a monumental battle with my wife by making the small gesture of bringing her a cup of tea.

Since Richie's suggestion had been so helpful I decided to ask him how I could correct my habit of keeping my body in a pike (an L instead of a 7) at the end of my swing. Richie said, "Take one of your own $100 bills and tuck it into the crease of your butt and it will solve your problem. You can't pike *and* hold on to the money. You are a Scot, so you will hold on."

This may have been the first time that being tight-assed helped me to make some beauty.

In my effort to create something of beauty on the trapeze I am sidetracked by comparing myself to others. Sometimes in the evening I watch videos of the great trapeze artists, scratchy films of the great flyers of the 1950s such as Tony Steele, Fay Alexander, or Reggie Armor, or film clips of contemporary troupes such as the Flying Gaonas or the Flying Vargas. Usually, I am filled with admiration for the skill and daring of the great trapeze artists and my more accomplished fellow flyers. But occasionally, some vile alchemy takes place in my ego and I begin to compare their consummate skill with my own awkward efforts and a dark mood overtakes me. I begin to envy rather than celebrate their achievement and to despair of my own.

I have learned from painful experience that comparisons are odious. Hours or days after I have judged myself as inferior, the current in my ego will reverse itself and I will begin to judge myself superior. I may not swing like Cadona, but I am a lot better than that overweight klutz Max who is younger than I am and has been practicing for years longer.

This cycle of comparison and judgment is Alice in Wonderland—"one pill makes you larger, one pill makes you small." It is being caught between two funhouse mirrors, one that makes you a giant and the other a midget. My ego keeps a trick ruler that I use to measure myself and others. One side shrinks inches to half-inches, the other stretches inches to two inches. Depending on whether I am in the mode of inferiority or of superiority, I turn the ruler to the stretch side, measure you, and find you are only three feet instead of six feet, or reverse the ruler when measuring myself so I am twelve feet instead of six.

This oscillation between feelings of inferiority and superiority, impotence and omnipotence (what the psychoanalyst

Karen Horney called the neurotic cycle), is such an accepted part of our culture of competition that it seems normal. We think sports and our economic system, which separate the winners from the losers, are a natural social extension of the evolutionary principle of survival of the fittest.

The practice of trapeze constantly reminds me of the folly of comparison and judgment. The moment I begin to evaluate myself in relationship to others, it really doesn't matter whether I judge myself inferior or superior. The up-down, superiority-inferiority, sadomasochistic mind game exiles me from my deepest experience of my own uniqueness.

I have to make a continual effort to excise the notions of competition, rank, and hierarchy from my thinking. They have no place within the silent dialogue with my self that I call my "spirit," for lack of a better word. The "still, small voice" of God never calls on me to be like another man. It appeals to me to rise to my full stature and fulfill the promise that sleeps within my being. In the long process of becoming the best possible Sam Keen, I constantly need to bring alertness, discernment, and discrimination to bear on the complexity of my experience. I need to be keenly aware of *my* takeoff, the rhythm of *my* swing, *my* timing, *my* dance with the catcher. In growing into the fullness of my promise, I need feedback. I do not need judgment. The Eleventh Commandment is: Thou shalt not compare thyself to others.

With my Promethean personality, I am in danger of sowing dissatisfaction as the vulture of old age nibbles at my liver if I fail to come to terms with my gifts and wounds, capacities and limitations. I need to remind myself frequently that in the art of flying trapeze, my ability and promise is small. Being chronologically challenged, I can only aspire realistically to do my small tricks elegantly. The best I can do is create miniatures.

On those days when my emotional life is in turmoil and I feel graceless, inept, and impotent, I sometimes climb to the pedestal, swing out over the chaos of the world, and make one flawless move. For a brief moment, a simple back-end uprise becomes a prayer in motion. My small gesture of mastery establishes a beachhead from which I launch an expedition to free myself from the dominion of incompetence, fear, panic, and worthlessness. With the feeling of the graceful uprise imprinted in my mind and body, I drop to the net and go about my business with the hope that the power in my gesture will invade and transform the dis-easy regions of my spirit. And sometimes it does.

The joy I feel in these moments of creating tells me that I am in the neighborhood of the sacred—the point where time and eternity meet. On those rare occasions when I get it exactly right I find myself thinking about Plato's idea of the pure, timeless forms or archetypes. When the trick clicks and the timing is perfect, for just a moment, I actualize the essential form—The Uprise—and it feels both right and perfect. For one fleeting moment, my small but elegant gesture partakes of the beauty of timeless perfection.

At breakfast I sat face-to-face with an amaryllis in full bloom. The dappled-pink trumpet blossom with its delicate emerald stem, backlit by the dawning sun, poured its beauty into my eyes, endowing my day with riches. I jumped up to the practice trapeze hanging from my living-room ceiling. I hung fully extended, filled my body with breath, pointed my toes, and slowly pulled myself into a knee hang. I tried to make the simplest movement beautiful. Sculpting a pure form in space, I chiseled away all that did not belong. I subtracted the carelessly protruding leg, the forward-drooping head, and brought everything into an elegant line. My moment of practice was more like cherishing a blooming amaryllis than it was like taking a risk.

A bonsai may be as beautiful as a redwood.

CHAPTER 7

A Fledgling Among the Eagles

When circus was real, flying was a religion.

Burt Lancaster
in the film *Trapeze,* 1956

Near the end of my first year of practice, an event occurred that was to open up a whole new world and expand my focus beyond the narrow range of my own practice. Ringling Brothers Barnum and Bailey came to the San Francisco School of Circus Arts. This unlikely event took place because our flying instructor was a friend of Peter Gold, the catcher for the Flying Vargas, and he invited all of the flyers and other performers to the school for an evening of food and fun. To our amazement a large crowd of miscellaneous acrobats and dare-devils showed up, lured by a chance to play on the flying tra-peze—something no one except designated flyers is permitted to do at Ringling. Suddenly, the large gymnasium that houses our school was a happy chaos of motorcycle riders and clowns bouncing on trampolines, and elephant riders and showgirls being introduced to the flying trapeze.

Near the end of the evening, an extraordinary performance was to take place. A kind of mutual show-and-tell. We were going to perform for them and they for us. Each of our fledg-lings was going to throw one trick to the catcher and attempt a return to the trapeze.

We were arranged in ascending order of skill with the best saved for the last. I was number 6 in the lineup (no longer the worst of the lot), and the trick I was going to attempt was a reverse knee hang to the stick, which requires the flyer to leave the pedestal with hands crossed, one hand facing each direction, turn around immediately on the outswing, get into a knee hang on the backswing, grasp the stick the catcher holds (since the flyer is approaching the catcher backward he is not caught by the wrists), swing back, and do a straight jump to the trapeze.

The scene, as you can imagine, resembled a group of beginning ballet students who had been asked to demonstrate their modest skills to members of the New York City Ballet. We were all dressed in our best tights and lycra outfits (I was wearing my electric blue for the occasion), and we milled about nervously chattering with one another, eyeing the audience that had gathered in the balcony to behold our wondrous performance. The circus music began and the master of ceremonies started his patter. When I heard him say something about "the oldest student in the circus school," I knew my time had come.

I began to sweat. I chalked my hands heavily to dry the moisture and climbed to the pedestal. The spotlight went on—at least I think there was a spotlight. And, for the first time, I was more terrified of the audience than I was of the trick.

Then it happened. I slipped into a stream of events and there was no time for self-consciousness. The last thing I remember is watching the catcher drop into his lock and shout, "Hep." At that point I vanished. I entered an ecstatic state of consciousness in which I was the action rather than the actor. The trick did itself and brought me along for the ride. When it was finished no one was more surprised than I, as I gave an awkward bow to the audience and returned to the sidelines, inordinately proud of myself.

I was still in a supercharged state when I sat down to watch my fellow flyers. As they did their tricks, small or large, it was as if each one was momentarily surrounded by a halo. The audience invested each with the power of self-transcendence that transformed a performance into something more. When the audience applauded and the performer bowed, it seemed very much like what happens in Buddhist countries when two people meet, bow to each other and say "Namaste" to acknowledge what is divine in the other. With the gesture of bowing I present this trick, this self, this life, as an offering. It is the only gift I have. The world is a stage, and Everyman a performer who may throw a single small trick in the cosmic circus.

By evening's end, all that remained of the party were a few passed-over casseroles of questionable contents from the potluck. A small group of students clustered around Peter Gold and the Flying Vargas troupe, and Bruno Vargas invited us to visit him backstage the next evening and to remain after the show to watch them practice.

Predictably, like children given free tickets to the circus, the chosen few appeared the next afternoon at the backstage door and were given passes. For several hours we hung out and talked, fascinated voyeurs of the mundane minutiae of the professional trapeze troupe's life. We watched the way they wrapped their fly bar, examined the leather grips they used to protect their hands, observed the exercises they did to warm up on their practice bar, pondering each detail as if it might contain some esoteric clue that would make us better flyers. I confess to an uncanny feeling that I had absorbed a bit of mana—magic power—by hanging from their practice bar.

We were so involved backstage that we missed the show until it was time for the Flying Vargas to perform. We filed in, took our seats, and waited.

What followed was exciting and confusing. Two trapeze troupes, the Flying Vargas and the Flying Alvarez, appeared simultaneously at opposite ends of the arena accompanied by drumrolls, um-pa-pa um-pa-pa waltzes, and swirling capes. They all climbed to their various perches and pedestals and began their performance of an impressive repertoire of tricks. By design, the acts were coordinated so that the audience at both ends of the Cow Palace were, supposedly, seeing the same tricks at the same time.

I expected to be thrilled and delighted. Instead I was disturbed by the impossible task of trying to pay attention to two intrinsically beautiful aerial ballets. My synapses were working overtime like a switchboard in a hurricane and the overall effect was one of aesthetic irritation.

There is something about the three-ring circus that is typically American. It is an extravagant form of conspicuous consumption, driven by the lust of the eye. It is MTV that bombards the senses with a collage of fast-changing images and produces sensory schizophrenia. It is the concupiscent drive for more, bigger, and better. Fundamentally, it is disrespectful. The manufactured cacophony and chaos of the three-ring circus does not allow the audience to pay attention to any individual artist.

My romance with the flying trapeze began with the circus of my childhood, but it had matured in the context of a school of circus arts where the emphasis was on creating something of beauty. Ringling Brothers left me in a state of cognitive dissonance, with questions about the meaning and context of the aerial arts. If the purpose of trapeze is to create something of beauty, and if something of beauty can only be appreciated when we give it our undivided attention, what is the context within which this art can best be practiced? Should it be in a theater as it was in the nineteenth century when it was first invented? Why are there no special arenas dedicated to the aerial arts, as there are to ice skating? Why is it not an Olympic event? Should there be Upward Bound centers where the art of flying is explored as a spiritual discipline? My budding practice had been animated by some unconscious need that had nothing to do with entertainment. I sensed that the meaning it would have in my life could not be understood within the context it was given in the three-ring circus. The art of living I was looking for was built on the principle "less is more," which is in direct contradiction to the principle "too much is not enough"—the underlying philosophy of MTV, the Mall, and Ringling Brothers.

What made the largest impression on me that day at the circus was not the tricks I saw but what I heard—the talk, the gossip, the stories of other flyers, other tricks, and other times. I had been so immersed in learning the basics of Trapeze 101, that it had not occurred to me that there was an enormous variety of aerial acts, past and present, that I might explore. Until I listened to the Vargas troupe compare their styles to others, I had no idea of who was doing what, where, and when. Who were the greats? What were the contemporary variations of the art?

My questions jolted me into awareness of the shallowness of my practice. Developing a practice in any art is not just a matter of doing. Learning an art involves entering a community, learning a language, a tradition, and standards of excellence. A would-be poet is initiated into the community of poets by learning the various languages of poetry, the rules governing the sonnet, and by studying Shakespeare and Shelley. A Zen student learns about sitting and meditation from a living master and by a disciplined study of the ancient teachers—the heroes of awareness. To deepen my practice I needed to search out the living masters, to collect their stories, to learn the lore and the traditions of the aerial tribe.

I left the circus that day with the determination to make pilgrimages to the places and people who could teach me about the state of the art, and with some recommendations of where I might begin. There was a consensus that Tito Gaona, who first did the blindfolded triple somersault and the double somersault with two full twists, and Miguel Vazquez, who first accomplished the "impossible" quadruple somersault, were the contemporary greats. Tony Steele, Fay Alexander, and Reggie Armor were reckoned to be the grand old gentlemen, and the Flying Cranes the most interesting recent innovation.

Once again, fortune smiled on me. With a little searching I discovered that the Flying Vazquez had just opened at Circus-Circus in Las Vegas for a long run, and that Tony Steele had retired and was living in Reno where the Flying Cranes had just begun a three-year run at the Reno Hilton. I was on an airplane quicker than you could say "Hep."

Las Vegas is an altered state of consciousness, a city where bad taste, flamboyance, and excess have been elevated to a profitable art and nothing is missing except modesty. Smack in the middle of the Strip was the first stop on my pilgrimage—Circus-Circus, host for more than thirty years to the great flying acts.

To reach the circus area, the pilgrim must first traverse the labyrinth. The casino floor consists of an acre or more of slot machines and blackjack tables arranged around intersecting circles, all covered with identical red carpet designed to keep the mass of gamblers disoriented and circulating endlessly. There are no clocks, no obvious ways to exit. The layout of the casino reminded me of the cartoon of the man sitting in a room with two doors, one labeled "No Entrance," the other "No Exit." I had the distinct feeling that I had entered into what Eastern philosophers called "a world of maya" that had been constructed by master architects of illusion. Here the ruling philosophy was "something for nothing." Once again, my quest had landed me in a very strange context, even stranger than the three-ring circus.

After three attempts, I found my way to the circus area, which contained carnival booths where the lucky might win a stuffed animal or other trinket and a small stage where various circus acts were presented throughout the day. Over the entire area hung a net and a trapeze rig where the Flying Vazquez did their three daily shows.

I arrived just in time to see Miguel; his wife, Rosa; Juan, his brother and catcher; and his twelve-year-old daughter, Victoria, walk into the arena to the accompaniment of the fanfare and swirl their capes as the master of ceremonies announced "The Flying Vazquez." I watched, full of anticipation, as they each took their warm-up swings. At last, I was going to see the quadruple somersault performed by Miguel Vazquez, the first man in history ever to accomplish it. Miguel forced out effortlessly, his body like an arrow shot high into space, glided back, whipped up into his set, broke hard, and soared into a double layout. After reaching the hands of his brother, he returned to the bar with a double pirouette. His every movement—a willow bending in the wind—was a blended essence of delicacy, power, and grace. It was easy to see why he held the most honored position in the modern pantheon of flyers. The perfection of his art was so dazzling he transcended the context of the casino, and I found myself thinking of the sacred image that is at the heart of Buddhism—the lotus blossom rising out of the polluted pond.

Victoria followed, with a simple knee-hang catch and return. In rapid succession, Miguel did a double twisting layout, Rosa did a double somersault. I was all geared up to witness my first quad when the master of ceremonies announced with fanfare that Miguel would now attempt "the legendary triple." After he completed the triple, as if it was child's play, the troupe did "the difficult and dangerous" passing leap and I realized that I wasn't going to see the quadruple somersault. They all did their dismounts to the net, and the show was over. Six minutes from beginning to end. I was disappointed because, even though I had never seen a more graceful flyer than Miguel, I had expected to see a more extended performance.

I followed the troupe into the dressing room, my mind

crammed with questions: Do you still have fear? Where is the edge for you? What is the best and the worst part about being a flyer, a catcher? Are there days when you can't focus, when your timing is off, when you lose your nerve? Do you ever have anything that seems like a religious or spiritual experience, a moment of transcendence, a feeling that you are taken over, moved? What contemporary flying acts do you most admire?

I opened the conversation by asking Juan how and when they had begun flying. "We were from a circus family," he replied, "and we had both a bar and a trampoline act. When I married Patricia, who was a flyer, my brothers and I decided to start our own flying act because that's where the money was. We heard that Tony Steele had a flying rig for sale so we drove to Elkhard, Indiana, and bought it. We stayed there for a few days, and Tony worked out with us and gave us pointers. You have to realize how unusual this was, because a guy who does a flying act doesn't want another flying act springing up. Tony was a complete flyer, he did all the big tricks but he was very generous in helping us get started. After that we were our own teachers. We had seen the Flying Gaonas and were awed by Tito's double twisting somersault, his blindfolded triple, and his dismount rebound from the net to the catcher's trapeze; we watched the old films of Alfredo Cadona; but we developed our own style. By the time he was fourteen Miguel had mastered the triple. Then, in 1982 Miguel became the first person ever to complete what had always been considered the impossible trick—the quadruple somersault to the hands of a catcher."

"And then," I said to Miguel, who had up until this point remained silent, "you missed the quad 251 times in a row before you finally caught it in a performance. What went through your mind? What kept you going after so many misses?"

"The quad wasn't that important to me. The press took some notice of it and Ringling Brothers paid me a bonus each time I caught it, but I got tired and bored after missing it a lot. But I didn't get desperate because I was only sixteen,'' Miguel replied in a low-key manner I was to discover was characteristic.

''Why didn't I see the quad today?'' I asked.

''We don't do it any more,'' Juan replied. ''The average American audience can't tell the difference between a triple and a quad, so we quit doing it. Now we stick to the classical flying trapeze.''

''I noticed that the crowd here at Circus-Circus was pretty jaded and unresponsive. Juan tried to get them to clap and work up some enthusiasm but he wasn't too successful. What is it like for you to perform before such an audience?'' I asked.

Miguel responded. ''I used to need the audience; I fed off their energy. When the flying trapeze act begins in the circus everyone sits quiet and watches—even the vendors. But here the audience is dead. So I block everything out—the casino, the noise. I still have my discipline and I try to make the act beautiful, because that is what catches people, but now I take it more like a job.''

''Are you trying anything new?'' I asked

''No,'' Miguel replied. ''I am pretty satisfied. I accomplished everything I set out to do. I completed more than two thousand quads. I tried a four-and-a-half but more for fun. It would be possible if I went after it, but my desire wasn't there to do more.'' Juan added, ''I want to teach my kids and catch them for another ten years. I will be fifty-eight by then and that's enough.''

''Do you still have fear?'' I asked.

''No,'' Miguel replied. ''I am a Christian and I believe in the Lord. This is my daily strength, and everything I have accomplished is from the Lord.''

''I don't have fear,'' Juan adds, ''but I am always aware that what we do is dangerous. Here at Circus-Circus if you miss the apron and fall out of the net it is fifty feet to the casino floor. So, if flyers come crooked I am not going to try to catch them because I could lose them in the apron. Every time I go up I ask the Lord to help my brother and my daughter, and I have an angel that protects us.''

"Who are the flyers and flying acts you admire?"

"I still believe that Cadona was one of the greatest flyers who ever lived. We have all learned from him. And for me, Tito Gaona is one of the greats. For a while trapeze acts were improving. I was the first to do full twisting triples and the quad and people looked at our videos and learned from them. But now things are stuck . . . no improvements," Miguel replied.

"What about the innovations in the Cirque de Soleil or the Flying Cranes?" I asked.

"The innovations catch the eye and the audiences like them because they don't know what they are seeing. What the Koreans or Russians do kills the classical flying trapeze. I can do what they do in two months. They have good choreography—they don't do hard tricks," Miguel said.

Juan chimed in, "Even when they do the quad they have a longer rig and longer cables on the catcher's trapeze so it makes it much easier."

I had heard about the brilliance of the new troupes but knew so little about them I didn't know what to reply. I remembered that Bruno Vargas had said, "The Flying Cranes act isn't real trapeze," and I couldn't help wondering whether these judgments were nothing more than a reflection of the perennial arguments between traditionalists and innovators.

As we talked further, I noticed a sense of disappointment growing in myself. Somehow, it had never occurred to me that the most high flying of all the angels would ever get tired, bored, or be content to rest on his laurels. How could trapeze become a routine day at the office? Miguel and Juan were slipping out of the category of heroes in which I had imprisoned them and becoming real human beings. I was lamenting the loss of my illusions. I had imagined that a great trapeze artist would live continuously in the feeling of ecstatic freedom that I experienced in my rare moments of flight. But, like me, they were ordinary persons who only occasionally soared beyond their quotidian existence. Very normal. I felt a bit like the reporter who asked a famous love goddess about her, supposedly, exciting amorous life only to be told, "It's nothing but sex, sex, sex, day in and day out."

By now it was late afternoon, and I had been invited to share a practice hour with Juan and his daughters at 5 P.M., so I excused myself, went to my room, and changed into my tights. When I returned, the spotlights and arena area were dark, but hoards of patrons still crowded into the carnival booths, trying their luck at various games.

Miguel no longer practices, so the hour session was dedicated mostly to Juan's daughters, Victoria and Veronica. As I climbed up to the pedestal I played with the fantasy that the unknowing gamblers who stopped to watch the practice imagined I was a retired trapeze artist just trying to keep in shape. I did my best swings, force outs, turnarounds, and returns to the board, uprises, hip circles, and falls to the net. Occasionally, Juan would shout a suggestion to me, but the serious business of the afternoon was Victoria's double somersaults, which she practiced again and again until her hands were sore. Like any teenager, she was ready to be done with the work, but her parents kept her at it until she was on the verge of tears.

As I watched the Vazquezes practice, I began to understand something that had puzzled me.

From my reading and my watching of old videotapes, I knew that the repertoire of tricks performed by past trapeze artists numbered in the dozens. During what circus historian Steven Gossard characterizes as the "era of reckless innovation in the aerial arts," which began in 1859 when Jules Léotard swung from one trapeze to another in the Cirque Napoléon in Paris (wearing the first "leotard"), there were many kinds of trapeze acts. Trapezes were hung from the underside of hot-air balloons, or on moving horse-drawn floats, or high above theater audiences. There are accounts of acts in which a man did headstands on a swinging trapeze while juggling, and of at least one act that featured swinging bears who supposedly did forty-two tricks. Flyers somersaulted from a trapeze to a vertical rope forty feet away. For a while there was a craze for flying through paper or burning hoops, sometimes with knives protruding. The great leap forward came in the 1880s with the flying return act in which a flyer goes from trapeze to catcher and back to the trapeze. Most of what we have come to identify as the classical tradition of trapeze as it is embodied in circus performances was created by Alfredo Cadona.

Why, I wondered, do the majority of modern flying acts repeat the same seven or eight tricks? In the typical circus act, each flyer takes a warm-up swing or two. Then come the "easy" tricks—the plange, the splits, the single layout, the heels-off—often performed by a woman or a fledgling flyer. Next come some combinations of difficult tricks—a double layout, a double twisting layout, a double-and-a-half to a legs catch. The climax of the act always includes two tricks. The first is inevitably introduced as "the legendary triple somersault to the hands of the catcher" and is performed by the senior flyer who is sometimes blindfolded. The second is always announced as the "difficult and dangerous" passing leap. Occasionally, one of the handful of elite flyers will attempt the quadruple somersault—the quad. After each trick, the flyer and the rest of the troupe "style," open their arms wide, and wait for applause. And then, less than seven minutes after it begins, the act ends. The catcher dismounts to the net; each flyer leaves the platform with a trick that ends with multiple bounces and twists in net; the troupe bows to the audience and exits the arena.

The uniformity is not because modern flyers are less skill-ful. To the contrary, Miguel Vazquez is every bit as good as "the great Cadona." The answer must lie in the conservative power of family and tradition. Of the seventeen trapeze groups that the circus magazine *Bandwagons* listed as having performed in the 1996 season, all but two are Hispanic. While American circuses as a whole have become more cosmopolitan with the influx of Soviet performers and the Canadian Cirque de Soleil, the flying trapeze has remained a Hispanic specialty. If you were to trace the genealogies of contemporary Hispanic flying acts, you would find an intricate tribal web of families who have intermarried. Should a flyer or catcher get injured, there is usually a brother, sister, or cousin somewhere on the circuit who can be counted on to fill in at a moment's notice. Further to the point, in circus families the children are taught the tradi-tional tricks by their parents and initiated into the act while they are still very young. What we have come to think of as the classical trapeze act, the repertoire of tricks and the standard rig, has persisted because of that much praised virtue—family values.

By the time practice was finished, I was tired, happy, and full of images and impressions it would take a long time to digest. I said my good-byes and returned to my room. After a hot bath, I descended to the casino, donated $10 to the slot machines, had dinner, took a walk along the neon avenue, and retreated to my room.

As I lay in bed savoring the experiences of the day, my mind began to free associate and throw some wild tricks. I was thinking about Miguel's triple somersault when, unaccountably, I saw superimposed over the pattern inscribed in space by the triple, the figure of a snake curled three times around itself.

The composite image baffled me. What kind of puzzle was

my mind presenting me? What possible relationship was there between a triple somersault and a coiled snake?

I no sooner asked the question than my friend Joseph Campbell appeared and offered me a clue. Once again, I heard the lecture I had heard a dozen times during the years we did seminars on mythology together. "The triple spiral is the ancient symbol for the ascending journey of consciousness. In the mystical meditation of Tantra, as it was practiced in Buddhism, the life force, the sexual energy, the power of consciousness— the kundalini energy—was symbolized by a snake curled three times lying at the base of the spine. The path to enlightenment, to spiritual consciousness, involves a continual unwinding and letting go of constricting notions of the self as a skin-encapsulated ego."

I can't say that Joseph's clue helped me solve the puzzle. If anything, it made it more complex. The link between trapeze and enlightenment, at best, seems tenuous if not ludicrous, but as I simmered and thought about it more, it occurred to me that at least three times in the course of a lifetime a man or a woman, like a snake shedding its skin, must lose one identity and gain another—at childhood's end, at the conclusion of maturity, and with the approach of old age and death. To move away from fear and grasping to the awareness that the self is at one with the energy and mind that informs the cosmos requires that we suffer three ego-deaths and celebrate three rites of passage. Maybe the journey of the soul, of *my* soul, is a legendary triple somersault.

At any rate, when exhaustion finally ushered me into that parallel world not governed by time or gravity, I dreamed I had only recently managed to complete the single layout somersault and was frantically trying to throw the triple—and failing. My teacher kept yelling at me, "Drive higher, spin faster, open up sooner, trust more and don't be so afraid of falling."

It was an exhausting night. I was happy to wake in the morning, have an expresso, hop on an airplane, and begin the second stage of my pilgrimage, which would take me to Reno.

The business of glitz, glitter, and gaming in Reno is a faux diamond in a real gold setting. The surrounding mountains provide a context that makes the city seem a modest size and reduces the casino area, and Circus-Circus where I was staying, to a single bright point on the landscape.

I had an appointment for breakfast with Tony Steele about whom I knew very little except that he was one of the most famous flyers of the last generation, now sixty years old and retired, and everyone spoke about him with both respect and affection. As a rule, great flyers are not great talkers, but Tony was the exception. All it took was an opening question about his career, and he began to tell stories that initiated me into the living tradition of trapeze and helped me weave together the history of the era between 1951 and 1986 when he traveled with every major circus in America and Europe before settling down to do daily performances in Circus-Circus and, finally, retiring. He told me about the time when he and Fay Alexander were flying at Ringling Brothers and were both trying (and failing) to complete the triple. Later, Fay Alexander was to do the actual flying in the Burt Lancaster film *Trapeze,* which dramatized the quest for the triple.

Near the end of our breakfast when the waitress seemed to be hurrying us along, I asked him about his wife Lilly's part in the Flying Steeles. An avalanche of stories poured out about their thirty-eight-year romance, their travels, their long life together, and her death from lung cancer nine months before. With eyes awash and his leprechaun face a mask of loneliness, he told me (unconvincingly), "I am gradually getting over the worst of the grief," and then he changed the subject. "I just started to get back in shape and I have built a small rig in my side yard. Why don't we go out and practice together?"

I gathered some fellow trapeze addicts who had joined me in Reno from their rooms in the hotel and we sandwiched ourselves into a minicar like a bunch of clowns.

The rig that sat beside Tony's trailer was a miniature that looked as if it had been constructed by Rube Goldberg out of a network of pipe and hardware clamps. The pedestal, which was about five feet from the ground, allowed a flyer to reach a trapeze that was hung from a limb of a convenient tree. At the far end of the rig, about twenty feet from the pedestal, there was a superstructure of pipe from which hung a cradle for the catcher. Because the whole apparatus was too low to the ground to accommodate a net, a system of pulleys and ropes hung from the tree, providing the only safety in case the flyer missed a trick.

Tony buckled himself into the safety belt, took a couple of test swings, and did a shoot over the bar. He was short, but the safety lines saved him from falling. The next one was perfect. Scott Cameron, the chief catcher from the San Francisco School, caught him, and Tony did a half-turn and returned to the bar. For the next couple of hours, we continued our high jinks on the low rig until everyone was tricked out and pleasantly sore. Tony was radiant. While we had tea and cookies in his trailer, he kept telling us that this was the most fun he had had since Lilly died.

We had to rush back to Circus-Circus to see the afternoon performance of the Flying Pages who had added to their (otherwise) traditional act a top catcher who stands on a small platform anchored by a safety belt directly above the traditional catcher on the swinging catch trap. After the performance we adjourned for supper and a rest because we planned to practice with the Pages after their last show at 10:45 P.M.

When the circus area closed for the night, a mixed congregation of flyers gathered on the sidelines to practice, watch, and kibitz. Vil Golovko, the creator and catcher for the Russian troupe the Flying Cranes, had come over from the Hilton because the Cranes had no performance that evening. The Flying Poemas, a group from Argentina who alternated with the Pages as the featured attraction at Circus-Circus, appeared from someplace and hung around. Tony Steele entertained us with corny vaudeville jokes and showed us how he uses his ventriloquist dummy to flip the bird to rude motorists who cut him off in traffic. Everyone shared trapeze lore, gossip about who is doing what tricks, comparing the intricate moves they make to accomplish various tricks. Luiz Poema regaled us with a description of a Mexican flying act in which chimpanzees had been trained to do the triple somersault, the passing leap, and other tricks. Tony compared the monkey's style to Jill Pages's. Jill, not to be outdone, claimed superiority over the chimps because she returns from the catcher with a double pirouette.

It was 1 A.M. and my body was a mixed cauldron of excitement and fatigue before I got a chance to practice. On the platform I handed the trapeze to Tony who swung out, returned, dropped the trapeze early, fell onto the board, grasping it with both hands as if he was out of control. He pulled himself around to the back and then fell to the net with arms flailing and mighty cries of disaster. Everyone laughed. The old clown can still work the audience with the klutz number. When my turn came I was more than usually nervous. New rig. An audience of experts. I swung a few times to warm up and dropped to the net. It was soft and nearly enveloping, too squishy to do any flips or fancy falls. My second turn I did an uprise and a sloppy hip circle and got some applause, which was more for the effort of "a man my age" than for my skill. Tony, five years my junior, twice attempted and once succeeded in throwing a forward somersault to the catcher and doing a pirouette return to the bar. The first time I attempted to come back to the board my rhythm was off and I crashed into the underside and bloodied my shins. Humiliated, I swung back out and dropped to the net. My second attempt was no more successful. The third attempt, I swung up and released the trapeze but didn't push it hard enough to be retrieved on its return flight—a definite breach of etiquette. I watched, embarrassed, as the arc of the pendulum shortened with every swing. When it was six feet beyond normal reach, Tony dove out, grabbed it, pumped up his swing, and returned to the board. Amazing. I threw a knee hang to Willy Pages but did not return to the trapeze because my half-turn to the bar was still too awkward to do without safety lines.

Sometime after 2 A.M. we finished practice and sat around talking. Vil said in a whisper, as if such sentiments should be uttered only in a reverent hush, "It is a great atmosphere here tonight." And it was. Clearly, this was a community of respect, admiration, and delight. It was touching to see the esteem accorded Tony Steele, the elder of the tribe, everyone's delight in his presence, and sensitivity to his grief. Jill admired Tony's T-shirt—an ancient Cranes shirt Vil had given him—so Tony stripped it off and gave it to her. A potlatch of shirt exchange resulted. I gave Vil my favorite Verve climbing shirt, and he gave me his black T-shirt.

At the dead end of the lively day, I made my way through the lower casino where lights were flashing and slot machines were being fed by loyal subjects who hoped against experience to enter suddenly into the kingdom of the lucky. In my room I took a quick shower and fell exhausted into bed.

As I was drifting into sleep, I reviewed the events of the last few days. Watching the great professional trapeze artists at Circus-Circus had given me an appreciation of the more intricate tricks that make up the contemporary repertoire: tricks with code names like the double-double (double-twisting double somersault), the double-cutaway (a double forward somersault with the flyer's back to the catcher, completed by grabbing a bar held out by the catcher), or the triple-double (that would forever remain, not only beyond my capacity, but beyond the ability of the average audience to distinguish).

As in so many modern sports and professions, the degree of technical difficulty has become the index by which we judge excellence. I can't help thinking that something important, call it charisma or heart, is lost when the standard for ice skaters, for instance, is how expertly they perform the double lutz or triple toe loop. While I was amazed at the double-twisting doubles, I found myself longing to see the great masters perform simple tricks in a masterly fashion.

There is a shaggy Zen story in which two disciples are bragging about the miracles their masters can perform. "My master can walk on thin air," says one.

"That is nothing to brag about," the other replies. "My master can walk on the earth, can eat when he eats and sleep when he sleeps." I am most interested in the beauty of simple acts, of seeing the ordinary performed with extraordinary charisma.

During those few days I had been included in a community of celebrants, an ecclesia of the air, gathered from the corners of the earth into an improbable tabernacle. I remembered the philosopher Robin George Collingwood's definition of community as a place where those who know teach those who wish to learn. There was a conspiracy there—a breathing together—a high flying companionship, an appreciation of excellence, a mutual admiration, a generous sharing of knowledge.

I turned toward home with a sense of belonging to a new tribe. I had met some of the heroes, teachers, and companions, who would sustain my enthusiasm, and encourage me in my efforts to become a flyer. I knew there would be many more places and people I would visit on my pilgrimage. I would return to Reno before long to see for myself what manner of phenomenon was this upstart group of Russians—the Flying Cranes. But for now, with my vision broadened, I was ready to return to my daily practice.

CHAPTER 8

The Art of Falling

Ashes, ashes, all fall down.

I hadn't been back from my circus journey for more than a week before I took my first bad fall. I suppose the memory of the beautiful flyers I had seen filled me with excessive enthusiasm and caused me to overreach. I had been doing simple back drops to the net for several months but had never attempted to throw tricks to the catcher without the protection of the safety lines when I, impulsively, decided that I was going to do a return without the lines.

Fear and excitement struggled for supremacy as I took off from the pedestal and went to the catcher, but the instant I turned and leaped for the return bar fear triumphed. I went totally blank, froze in midair, plummeted to the net feet first and landed in a twisted standing position. To keep myself from bouncing out onto the ground, I immediately pitched forward and grasped the net. When I tried to get up I realized I had wrenched my back, and a further inventory revealed that I had lacerated the skin on a few fingers. I could tell from the quality and the quantity of pain that I would not be flying for a week or so.

In my premature enthusiasm to fly free, I had violated a fundamental principle. Learn the fall before the trick; prepare for failure. From the moment when a fledgling accomplishes the first free fall, progress in flying and falling go hand in hand. I had come to the point where I could not risk flying higher until I had mastered the art of falling.

I was, and still am, painfully awkward and slow in learning to make the controlled midair twists and turns that are necessary for a safe landing in the net, if and when I miss a trick. After I recovered from my bad fall, I spent many months focused on developing a kinesthetic awareness of where my body is in space at all times. Sometimes I would swing from the bar and do a simple back flip—kick forward, back, forward, release the bar, tuck, slap my knees, open and fall to the net on my back. As I rotated in midair, I focused on the changing position of my body in relation to a fixed point—ground zero, the net. At first, my awareness was like a jerky old film that was missing many of the frames. I could visualize the beginning and the end, but about the time I slapped my knees, I blacked out, lost consciousness of my rotation, and regained awareness just before I hit the net.

Consider the difficulty of twisting, turning, changing directions in midair, or midlife. In the first place, the art of twisting and falling is not one of those leisurely spiritual practices like Zen archery, the Japanese tea ceremony, or walking meditation. It is all well and good to talk about "going with the flow, letting go, becoming purposeless," but if you don't turn correctly in the instant you have available and fall on your back, you aren't going to miss the target or spill the tea, you are going to get hurt. Study the movements of Tito Gaona and you will see that mastering the art of falling is a matter of "grace under pressure," as Hemingway said about the great bullfighters. It is a worldly rather than a monastic discipline.

In midair, as in midlife, the necessity to change is often thrust upon us. When we miss the trick, get fired, divorced, sick, or depressed, our trajectory is already set by our past habits. It is difficult to get the leverage to change. Unless you develop the art of turning while falling, the forces pushing you from the past carry you in a predetermined direction.

Since I am in what is considered late middle age, I am about to tumble into a new stage of life. My youngest child is about to leave the nest; the dynamics of my marriage are changing; my professional and erotic drives are slowing down; I am edging toward the time when I will no longer be able to deny that I am "getting old"; my days are being compressed by the approach of death. To accomplish my final tricks I need to learn how to fall gracefully. To date, I have been better at holding on than letting go.

In physics, the problem of change while in motion is stated thus: If outside vectors are absent, the trajectory of a body in motion can only be changed by the reconfiguration of the body itself.

How do we break the trajectory of our lives and do something new? When we are overwhelmed by change, it seems as if we are in an impossible situation, like astronauts trying to maneuver in zero gravity where everything just floats. But in fact an astronaut, unlike a flyer, has something solid against which to push. As astronaut Ed Mitchell explained to me, "without something to push against, an astronaut can fold and unfold an arm or leg but cannot generate momentum to rotate the body. However, the slightest push against the space capsule creates a great force since, without gravity, there is no resistance to slow down the motion." At the other extreme, a parachute jumper in free fall can accomplish all manner of mile-high acrobatic high jinks because the massive wind resistance generated by an accelerating falling body provides a counterforce against which one can push. A trapeze flyer uses the momentum initiated by the swing and the push off the bar; but once in midair, the unfolding of the ballet depends on an inner compass and the

ability to sculpt the body in space by the most subtle adjustment of an arm, a leg. Tuck tightly to spin, open out to stop
the rotation.

Many great trapeze artists have no idea how they do what
they do. On my recent journey I asked both Jill Pages and Tony
Steele about turning and falling. They are obviously world-class
experts, having survived many missed triple-and-a-half somersaults in which they approached the net head first and had to
tuck and turn immediately to land safely in the net.

"When you miss a trick, how do you land safely? How do
you remain aware of your position in space as you contort your
body through a series of elaborate rotations and twists?" I
asked.

"I do it all by feeling," Jill explained. Then, as an after-
thought she added a sentence that struck discouragement into
my heart. "Some people are cats and some people aren't."

"I don't know. I just do it," Tony said. "Falling the right
way is an instinct; it comes naturally. I wear contact lenses and
I can't see a lot when I am flying. There is something very
occult about initiating a spin in midair. Something I can't explain. It is all about torque and vectors. When you come off the
bar when you are doing a double twisting layout, you throw the
bar behind your head to get a little more momentum. You
begin a revolution and then convert that energy into a twist
using little shoulder movements, and stop the rotation by letting an arm go out."

It is clear that the great flyers have always been great fallers.
The ability to convert a failed attempt into a graceful fall is the
essence of creativity. Thomas Edison failed a thousand times
before inventing the lightbulb. If you aren't failing frequently it
is because you are too timid or too stuck in your rut to try
anything new and risky.

One of the early legendary flying acts at the turn of the
century was composed of Earnest Clarke, the flyer, and Charles

Clarke, the catcher. Without any third person to return the trapeze, these brothers mastered a double somersault and a pirouette return. In his *Big Top Rhythms,* Irving Pond reports an interview in which he asked Earnest about falling.

"Earnie, you must have had a few falls into the net before you got that act to perfection. Five hundred, say?"

"Well," he answered, "five hundred would hardly be a circumstance. We tried it at each and every rehearsal for a year and no fewer than ten times at each rehearsal before ever our hands came together (and every try meant a fall into the net). Then we caught and held. In three and a half years more we reached the point where we thought we would be justified in presenting it in public. More than two thousand falls; and then three and a half years before it was perfected."

I am reluctant to accept Jill Pages's doctrine of corporeal determinism because I am not a cat and I am loath to be condemned to dwell forever in the kingdom of the dogs. I rebel against the Calvinistic notion of double predestination—divine grace as the birthright of some and disgrace of others. I recognize genius when I see it, and Jill is a Georgia O'Keefe with a palette of aerial hues and Tony an Einstein of the air. But I suspect that much of their kinesthetic superiority and extraordinary grace came by way of nurture rather than nature. It is likely that both did acrobatics, gymnastics, and trapeze since they were children and just can't remember the time before they learned what they are calling "an instinct."

Since permanent change is here to stay, to accomplish anything bold and beautiful in the firmament of time we must learn to change direction and fall gracefully.

Fate sets each of us on a given trajectory—we are born male or female, American or Vietnamese, robust or fragile, endomorphs or ectomorphs, with high or low IQ, to caring or cruel parents, in wealth or poverty, and so on. Freedom arises from our ability to change those things within ourselves and in our environment that can be changed, and to adapt creatively to those that cannot. Like a diver or a flyer in midair, we change the trajectory of our destiny by discovering our inner guidance system—the internal torques and vectors.

What we call wisdom is the learned ability to maneuver our way through life gracefully by consulting a wide variety of inner guidance systems or homing devices. As a flyer I must learn to trust my kinesthetic conscience, my inner gyroscope, my bodily sense of location and movement. To act in a moral way, I depend on conscience as the vector to be true to my best values. Compassion is the compass that keeps me on a kindly track in my relationship with others. My gastronomical conscience is my innate sense of what is most nourishing to my body. My aesthetic conscience is the awareness of the colors, textures, forms, and patterns that are pleasing to my senses. My sexual conscience is that part of my desire system that draws me to creative and fulfilling sexual experiences. My geographical conscience is the sense of place that reminds me it is most fitting for me to live in the presence of trees on which I may swing and streams in which I may play. My vocational conscience is my calling to develop and share my most meaningful gifts and talents.

It is only by remaining in touch with the whole range of inner guidance systems that I can determine when I am moving in a potentially destructive trajectory. The dis-easiness of any of my multiple consciences is a sign that I need to make midair corrections. Stomach upset? Listen to my body and change my diet. Has my work become routine and empty? Consult my vocational vector to find where I have gotten offtrack.

I have to proceed on the assumption, or call it faith, that I have some measure of control over the trajectory of my life. Clearly, my genes did not predispose me to the feline graces.

Nevertheless, I work and hope. I will turn my head to the left, duck my shoulder, and roll as I fall, a thousand more times until it becomes instinctual. I will learn to use a dangling arm or extended leg as a trim tab to adjust my trajectory. I look forward to the time when I will be at peace with continual change and the transitoriness of life, and I will have become an excellent faller.

Three times since I started trapeze, different friends have sent me the Gary Larsen cartoon that shows a dog on a tight-rope riding a unicycle while juggling. The caption beneath says, "High above the hushed crowd, Rex tried to remain focused. Still, he couldn't shake one nagging thought: He was an old dog and this was a new trick." Maybe I will ask Gary to draw another cartoon inspired by a recent event in my family. My daughter Jessamyn came home from school to find her father repeatedly dropping her cat from a height of three feet onto the sofa to see how it turned in midair.

"What are you doing with my kitty?" she asked.

"I'm studying to be a cat," I replied.

Of course, falling cats can only twist, turn, land on their feet, and go about their normal business. Falling humans can twist, turn, land on a net, and bounce again into the air. We have the gift of freedom, of improvising, of beginning again.

When I tell someone I practice the flying trapeze, the most common question I hear is, "Do you use a net?"

"Always!" I answer.

Originally, flying trapeze acts were done over water, mat-tresses, or sawdust, but since fishing nets were modified a cen-tury ago, the net has become a standard feature of all flying trapeze acts. High-wire walkers—such as Charles Blondin who crossed the gorge over Niagara Falls or the Great Wallendas who walked the canyons between tall buildings—and single-swinging-trapeze artists work without a net. Not flying trapeze acts.

Initially, I thought of the net as nothing more than a safety device that would protect me if I could manage to fall correctly on my back, seat, or stomach. As I gained skill in twisting, turning, and landing, however, I realized it was more than a concession to human fallibility; it was also a platform from which to launch new flight. A modern nylon net is essentially a large trampoline that invites a flyer to convert a fall into a re-bound trick—a somersault, a suicide dive, a high balletic leap. Professional trapeze troupes always end their acts with dramatic dives or somersaults to the net. In fact, the trick that seems to delight audiences more than any other is one introduced by Tito Gaona in which he plummets to the net, bounces very high, somersaults, and lands seated on the catcher's trapeze.

Gradually, I am learning to enjoy the creative possibilities of the rebound. I suppose there are exceptional men and women whose lives are an unbroken series of successes, but for most of us the ascending path is punctuated by times of descent, downfall, and depression. My failures have taught me there is always a second chance. What I have managed to create after falling has often turned out to be better than the trick I planned. Failing gives fallible human beings the chance to start over. This is why every man, woman, and society needs a safety net.

CHAPTER 9

The Outer Eye and Inner Vision

It is only after your eyes became a circus
that you can see your life as it really is.

Brooke Stevens
in *The Circus of the Earth and Air*

$Sometimes$ *the practice* of trapeze peeled
away the outer layers of my psyche and allowed me to look
more deeply into my self than I have been enabled to do by
either philosophy or psychotherapy. Twice in the last month,
my efforts to accomplish small physical movements have triggered some new self-knowledge. The trapeze rig, like an MRI
(magnetic resonance imaging) camera, showed me what lies
beneath my surface.

I was working on a pullover shoot, a trick that involves
taking off from the pedestal, swinging out to the end of the
pendulum while pulling myself up and over the bar so I am
supported on my down-stretched arms with the bar grazing my
hip bones, and on the second swing, as I reach the apex of the
pendulum, flexing my arms, pushing myself off the bar, and
flying over to the arms of the catcher. After numberless attempts I had finally learned all the pieces of the trick and put
them all together but was still failing to reach the catcher.
Sometimes, we managed to slap hands but my flight was always
too short and I fell to the net in the nose-plant position.

After the third failure of the evening, my teacher asked me,
"Where are you looking the moment when you leave the trapeze?"

"I'm not sure. I'll try it again and pay attention to what I am paying attention to."

My fourth attempt was also a failure but I did manage to catch a glimpse of my own eyes. They were focused broadly on the catcher who was coming up from below, and specifically on his outstretched hands. When I reported this, my teacher said, "Your problem isn't in the mechanics of the trick; it isn't in what you are doing; it is in where you are looking. Do everything exactly the way you are doing it, except look up toward the sky rather than down at the catcher. Forget the catcher and fly upward."

Fifth attempt. I shot off the bar with my arms and eyes pointed heavenward, like Superman trying to leap great buildings in a single bound. I never saw the catcher as he rose from somewhere beneath my point of vision and grasped my wrists.

Later, as I mulled over what had happened, it struck me that for an instant that evening the normal current of my psyche had reversed itself, allowing me to see that what had been holding me back was not a lack of physical prowess but my habitual stance in life. I am by nature, or nurture, an introvert. My tendency is to turn my vision inward and look down into myself, a tendency that is mirrored in the downward curve in my posture. I have the scholar's forward-slumping shoulders.

It is not accidentally that most trapeze artists are extroverts. They are an upward- and outward-looking tribe, optimistic by nature, not given to brooding on their failures or worrying unduly about the risks they are taking. They are doers rather than thinkers. Many of the best of them can neither explain how they do what they do or talk about the emotions and subtle experiences that accompany their flying. This, incidentally, is one of the reasons I was so readily welcomed into the aerial community. My awkward but enthusiastic efforts to fly coupled with my facility with language allowed me to translate the inarticulate poetry of motion into words, to give utter-

ance to the silent deeds of the aerial artists. Unlike most jour-
nalists, I did not ask dumb questions like, "Do you use a net?"
(In flying trapeze, yes; in single-swinging-trapeze, no.)

If, as the Swiss psychologist Carl Jung suggested, the task
we face in the second half of life is to develop our "inferior
function," the practice of trapeze seems the perfect antidote
for my introversion. It is good therapy for a recovering Presbyterian; it gets me out of myself.

Hard on the heels of the realization that where the eye
travels the body will follow came another revelation.

Flyers, like golfers, are always working to perfect their
swing. It is a bit like the Austrian dressage master who died at
eighty-seven, at which time his brother said, "It's a shame. He
was just beginning to get his seat." So, one day I was working
on my swing and force out and decided to call Tony Steele, who
was rapidly becoming my long-distance guru and consultant,
for some advice. I had hardly begun to describe my problem—I
couldn't generate enough height and power in my swing no
matter how much energy I put into it—when he gave me his
diagnosis and prescription.

"I noticed when you were in Reno and we were practicing
together that you have a lot of energy, determination, and
strength, but you don't extend and arch outward at the end of
your force out. You collapse and curve inward at the end of
your swing. To correct this, you have to fly proud. At the front
end, when you force out, extend your body up and away from
the trapeze bar and then level off with a slight arch in your
back. At the apex of your swing you should be where angels
fear to tread. At the back end, as you reach what seems to be
the apex, hold your head up like a proud or arrogant person,
and believe that you can go higher still. Plant in your mind the
image of a toreador. This will make you fly proud. Later on,
when you come to making your turns, either to the net or to
the catcher, imagine the toreador holding his cape as the bull

makes a pass. This image will make your body move proud as you turn and you will fall correctly in the net with your legs behind you, your chest out, and your chin tucked.''

"To fly proud.'' The phrase itself created in me a strong feeling of mingled anxiety and excitement. Why should such an innocent phrase and the image it evoked produce such a strong reaction? I'm enough of a student of Freud's to know there is always some treasure hidden beneath turbulence, so I let my mind take flight and free associate.

Proud. Pride. Pride goeth before a fall. Lucifer, the fallen angel, tried to fly too high. Arrogance. Conceit. Cockiness. Vanity. Damnation. Hell. Death.

Humble. The opposite of proud. Humility. Head bowed, as in prayer. Near to the ground. I learned at my parents' knees that pride was a sin and humility a virtue. My dad's last letter before he died quoted a passage from 1 Peter in which he took great comfort. "Humble yourselves under the mighty hand of God, that he may exalt you in due time: Casting all your care upon him; for he careth for you.''

When I was a child I was encouraged to choose between pride and humility. As a Christian I was supposed to be proud, because I was created in the image of God to be a magnificent individual, but was to remain meek, mild, and soft-spoken. Nietzsche was one of the few who understood how radically Christianity reversed or "transvalued'' the classical virtues and vices and turned pride into a sin. Even as a young professor of philosophy and the Christian faith, I was still struggling with this dilemma. One evening I was drinking beer with an old friend and shared my struggle with him. He responded, "Sam, I always thought arrogance was one of your few good qualities.'' I still love him for that.

It is discouraging for me to be confronted with the evidence that something deep in my body and psyche has not yet broken free of my childhood religion. My inner vision is still partially focused on achieving a false kind of humility and is fearful of healthy pride. That must be why I tremble with fear and excitement at the thought of "flying proud."

I unconsciously made the mistake of confusing pride with arrogance and humility with shame. The traditional posture of humility—the bowed head and bent knee—is not that different from the posture of shame. Look at images of the saints. How many examples do we have of robust, vital, erotic men and women who are proud rather than ashamed of their bodies? If we think of primal shame as a disease in which we hide within a demeaning sense of our smallness and insignificance, it is clear that primal pride must be a virtue. We are not meant to be less powerful, less beautiful, less erotic, or less creative than we are. To hide our magnificence under a facade of modesty is to allow shame to masquerade as humility.

To fly well I need to refocus my inner vision on the image of a proud and graceful body. Vision moves us more efficiently than willpower; we are more often drawn into the fullness of our being than we are pushed into it. Let your eyes and your imagination soar and your body will follow. The great power that propels us—the prime mover—is that inner vision of our best possible self we see with "the eye of the soul." As the acorn yearns to become an oak tree, we are drawn toward our ideal future by a magnetic force, an inner homing device. What the great spiritual traditions call hope is the veiled vision of our now and future unfolding. I need to let the image of the toreador creep inside me and re-form my body. Stand tall, breathe deep, plant my feet firm, keep my head level and my eyes skyward. Inhabit every cubit of my stature—no more, no less. Look up and out.

Over the last five years I have come to know some of the greatest trapeze artists of our era. At first glance, it would seem that these professional "heroes" who perform for the crowd must have enormous egos. They enter center stage amid fanfare, wearing tights and capes covered with spangles that glitter in the spotlight. After each trick they style, pose, await the adulation of the audience. Surely, they must be prime egotists, and "ego" (as most religious traditions teach) is something that must die in order for the "true self" to be born.

To my surprise, I discovered a marvelous amalgamation of seemly pride and modesty in most all of them. To begin with, overweening pride (what the Greeks called hubris) is not a common vice among professional trapeze artists because an arrogant flyer will very soon learn the literal truth of the biblical warning "pride goeth before a fall." The airborne community has a built-in discipline of truthfulness. Circus advertising may thrive on superlatives—the greatest, the only, the world-renowned, the bravest of the brave—but among the performers there are no inflated résumés. If you claim you can do the quadruple somersault, your word will be tested high above the arena in full view of the multitude. The best flyers in the world have a matter-of-fact honesty about their accomplishments that I find refreshing, especially when I remember my years as an editor of *Psychology Today* when I interviewed a gaggle of famous therapists, gurus, and religious leaders, all of whom proclaimed their brand of therapy or path to salvation to be *the* one and only true way.

There is something at play here that is a healthy correction to the traditional religious view of life. Great artists, whether on the trapeze or the theater, feel it is their *vocation* to give their best performance to their audience. They find their reason for being in giving delight. Tito Gaona, who is a very flamboyant flyer, told me that he learned about playing to and with the audience from his father's often-repeated saying: "The trick is not to pee, but to make the foam." Every time he performs, he picks out someone in the audience to please. His sizable ego is not destroyed but purified by sharing his gift. It is much like someone once said about Frank Sinatra: "No matter what you say about the man, when he started to sing he was honest."

I think we need a new word—*comjoyment*—as a companion to *compassion,* to remind us that our greatest gift to the world may be in sharing what gives us the greatest joy.

I recently did a benefit lecture for a worthy cause and the organizer of the event, knowing about my passion for trapeze, made me a belt with rhinestone spangles as a token of appreciation. I hope one day I will be modestly proud enough to wear it.

CHAPTER 10

The Sonoma Trapeze Troupe

*It is wonderful having to work for something and rely
on other people as a team to do it. I end up flying
with people with whom I wouldn't otherwise be associated
and trusting them with my safety and my life.*

Masha Nordby

One Saturday while I was sitting on the bench awaiting my next turn on the trapeze, I was wishing out loud that I had my own trapeze rig so I didn't have to travel into San Francisco twice a week. Stephan Gaudreau, the chief trapeze instructor, overheard me and suggested that if I would get a dozen students in Sonoma he would install his portable rig on my farm and teach classes there. How could I refuse? After a month of bulldozing and landscaping we were ready for the new era to begin.

If you were to come unexpectedly on the freestanding trapeze rig in the woods just across from my writing studio, it might appear to be a giant creature from a prehistoric age or some kind of apparatus for reviving signals from outer space—antennas for communication with the beyond. It is, in fact, simply a machine that allows human beings to fly without benefit of wings and to fall from great heights without injury. By modern standards, it is an extremely primitive tool with few moving parts and no motors, but, considered mythologically, it is a remarkable, almost mystical, device—the opposite of the Procrustean bed. It stretches body and soul enough to allow human beings to soar momentarily, but it does not induce the hubris that makes them believe they can fly to the sun, like

Icarus on wax-and-feather wings, or ascend to the throne of God on angelic ones.

Four pairs of spindly legs (crane poles), each joined at the top by a crossbar, are arranged to form a rectangular cube sixty-five feet long, thirty-one feet high, and twelve feet across that is held together and anchored to the ground by a dozen or more steel cables.

Next to the first crane, a narrow ladder leads up to what is variously called the platform, the pedestal, or the board, six feet long by eighteen inches wide, from which the flyers initiate their midair choreography. In back of the board hangs a ten-foot pole (the noodle), with a hook on the end that is used to retrieve the flyer's trapeze that hangs from twelve-foot steel cables from the second crane bar. The catcher's trapeze (the catch bar or catch trap) is hung from eight-foot cables from the third crane bar. Beside it hangs a thick rope the catcher climbs to reach his perch.

In the indoor arena in San Francisco, as in the circus, the platform and trapezes are hung from the ceiling rather than from freestanding crane bars, but the dimensions of the rig remain, essentially, the same.

Beneath the entire rig, a gauze-like net made of nylon forms an artificial floor eight feet above the actual floor and extends upward to form walls (aprons) on either end that close off the space behind the platform and behind the catcher to prevent injury should a flyer overshoot the mark in returning to the platform or be dropped by the catcher.

There is one further device, a set of safety lines (the "mechanic"), which is held by a trainer and connected to a safety belt, that allows a novice or an accomplished flyer to work on tricks without the risk of a bad fall to the net.

This simple superstructure with its steel bones and rope sinews forms the airy walls that contain the world of trapeze. Like a baseball diamond, a football field, a law court, or a ballet theater, it is a self-defined realm of meaning that has its own laws, its own language, its own history and traditions, and its own heroes. It is a playground, a field of dreams, a place of adventure for body, mind, and spirit, but its magic begins with ordinary stuff—pipes and cable and nylon.

Having a trapeze rig outside my studio door changed the entire nature of my practice. Any time I got tired of writing, I could cross the bridge to the playground. I knew it wasn't smart to practice by myself, but when it was late afternoon and the wind was rustling the leaves of the maples, I couldn't help slipping into the woods and swinging on the grapevines.

My advertisements in a local newspaper collected a dozen interested neophytes and created an instant trapeze school with the instructors from the San Francisco school teaching regular Wednesday and Sunday classes. Within a few months, a hard core of enthusiastic flyers gathered and we christened ourselves the Sonoma Trapeze Troupe and began to practice together several times a week. As in any community, we had a natural diversity of talents and timidities, and since we perfected different skills and learned different tricks, we became teachers to one another. I was the first to perfect the back-end uprise, which I taught to David who, in turn, taught me some fancy falls he had mastered. Occasionally, we had an official teacher, but increasingly we critiqued each other's moves and tricks, encouraged each other, and figured things out by trial and error. We collected and watched videos of great flyers and studied their techniques. We videoed and analyzed our practice sessions. The more we began to trust in the efficacy of our shared ignorance and wisdom, the more we each became "master" and "student." Unlike most spiritual communities, we killed the guru and learned by sharing our gifts with each other.

Practice gradually moved away from being a special event and became an integral part of our daily lives. As I followed a regular routine of stretching and warming up, the chronic pains in my arms and shoulders disappeared. Hanging and swinging on the trapeze became so comfortable that I felt out of sorts if I was deprived of it for a few days.

Climbing the ladder and standing on the board became no more fearful than standing on the ground, in large measure because our amateur troupe changed one of the sacred traditions of the tribe. For reasons that are obscure, the orthodox pedestal board is a twelve-inch sliver hung over an abyss and must accommodate three people, one or two of whom are in a constant process of taking off, landing, dropping return bars, and bowing to the audience. As all the members of our small troupe were in the early stages of mastering the basic turn-arounds and returns to the board, our efforts resembled nothing so much as adolescent buzzards trying to land on a twig. So we broke with tradition and made a thirty-six-inch-wide board on which four or five of us could congregate, encourage each other, and rescue our fellow flyers whose approach to the landing strip was either too short or too long. At first, our teachers railed and ridiculed our innovation. They sneered, ''The board is no place for comfort, or parties,'' and predicted that people would grow complacent and fall because the landing pad was too large. But, in time, the defenders of the old order embraced the novelty, especially after Tony Steele, who happened to be visiting one weekend, dignified our heresy by announcing to the congregation that he and his catcher Billy Woods once built a six-foot board that accommodated a sofa and an ice chest so they could stay up there all day.

Much of what our troupe practiced and learned that first year were the intangibles—flexibility, rhythm, and timing—rather than tricks.

Because I am lanky and male I had a problem with flexibility and rhythm. Had you watched me dance you would have seen that, like most plain vanilla men, I tended to be stiff through the middle and to compensate by a flurry of arm and leg motion. My momentum came more from my extremities than my center, a pattern that limited my flexibility and power in almost all the moves required for trapeze. A good flyer needs hips like Elvis and a spine like a black-snake whip. I, unfortunately, had the hips and spine of Gary Cooper in *High Noon* or Clint Eastwood in *Hang 'Em High*. No bend, no swing, no sway. It doesn't mean a thing if you ain't got that swing. I had no way to generate the lift and power necessary to propel myself into any of the big tricks. In both my swing and my break, my body was so unbending that I had virtually no back kick and therefore could not drive myself upward. To gain power I needed to extend the pendulum on both ends, to stretch back and reach forward.

Naturally (or rather, unnaturally), at first I tried to force myself to be more flexible. Bend, damn it, bend! When that didn't work, I began the not unpleasant discipline of studying the hips of our most lithe and lovely female flyer. For reasons having everything to do with gender, women tend to be more flexible than men and to move naturally from their center, from what the martial arts call the *kath* or *hara*. Gradually, ever so gradually, I learned to bend and lead with my hips, to move in a more powerful and womanly way.

With this increase in flexibility I began to get into the rhythm. As my swing lengthened, I felt the still point at the top, relaxed into the glide downward, and backed up with a snap. Instead of trying to power myself, I rode the pendulum, and let gravity do the work.

It is passing strange and marvelous: when you stop fighting gravity you discover grace. When I finally got the force out and the swing just right, there was a moment when I seemed to pass from an ordinary rate of motion into warp-speed. The momentum of the pendulum took over, effort gave way to grace, and the feeling I had was like the representation in *Star Wars* when the ship goes into hyperspace. Grace seems to be a kind of hypermotion in which we break through into another dimension. The fourth dimension?

I offer one bit of empirical evidence to substantiate my feeling that there has been a fundamental change in the rhythm of my being. A few months ago my wife and I were invited to a black-tie dinner and dance. I had accepted with reluctance and was surprised to notice that I was actually enjoying the occasion enormously. Late in the evening, full into the boogie, my wife looked at me quizzically and asked, ''When did you learn to dance like that?''

The new rig was changing everything because, as George Bernard Shaw said about marriage, ''it combined the maximum of temptation with the maximum of opportunity.'' As I began to practice more frequently, however, I found I was suffering from mood swings. September 11 was a perfect Indian summer day, and I was bright and energetic as a squirrel collecting acorns for winter. I sprinted up the ladder, tried new tricks, soared high and strong as if my chest were a helium balloon and my arms were stainless steel cables. September 12 was also a perfect Indian summer day, but I was down, dull, and depressed. No matter how hard I tried, there was no lift in my swing, no snap in my turns, no singing in my muscles. It may or may not be true, as William Blake said, that ''the path of excess leads to the palace of wisdom'' but on the trapeze it leads to fatigue, mistakes, and folly. A better guide is Aristotle who counseled the golden mean—balance and moderation.

I needed to learn to curtail my endless desire and accept the rhythm of my days. Like the prophets of the Dow, I dream of new daily highs and endless progress without depression or inflation. Young men, like stockbrokers, hope against all evidence that what goes up will stay up.

But the seasons of mind and body change, and there are days when I walk and faint, run and am weary, and am unable to rise up on the wings of eagles.

Gradually I cobbled together a rough barometer to help me assess my daily condition. Each day I monitor the rise and fall of several variables—the umph factor, the verve factor, the will factor, and the grace factor—to get a rough idea of how my soul-weather is changing. The interplay of these factors like atmospheric highs and lows and offshore winds governs the climate of the day.

The umph factor, the amount of raw energy I have on any given day, varies according to how much I had to eat and drink the night before, how much sleep I have had, how much I have exhausted myself by too much travel, work, or trapeze practice, and with the mysterious variation of seasonal rhythms. For me February, not April, is the cruelest month. Midwinter is the low ebb when the surplus energy I stored from summer and fall is depleted and I can only await the returning spring. Add to this the monthly fluctuation of biorhythms. Men do not, ordinarily, menstruate but something that is a kissing cousin to PMS strikes us—moods, minidepressions, unexplained energy crises, and (gasp) impotence.

The verve factor is the amount of nerve and courage I have on any given day. There are days when I find it easy to take reasonable risks, to experiment with tricks that are just beyond the edge of my competency. There are other days when somebody pulls the plug, the water starts to circle the drain, and I lose my nerve. The doldrums, a downdraft, a sinking of spirit. No élan vital. It is all too much. Why bother?

This condition has been called by many names: the Greeks labeled it melancholy; the Christians called it acedia and described it as the demon that walks at midday; the French philosopher Blaise Pascal called it ennui and thought it was the main symptom of a godless life; German philosophers described it as world-weariness; the English called it boredom and considered it the French disease. Once, it was simply the blues and it came from being on a lonesome road a long way from home. Lately, we have stripped it of spiritual significance, renamed it "depression" and promised to cure it with pills.

Whatever you call it, this demon lurks in the shadows ready to strike if I move too fast, work too much, or live without passion.

Alfredo Cadona called it "casting—the demon of the circus tent" and held it responsible for the death of many performers.

Casting, to the circus performer, is a purely psychological term. It has to do with that part of an instant when the mind seems to let go, to refuse longer to hold to the terrific burden of concentration which has been placed upon it. It is like a sharp knife struck suddenly against a set of tightly drawn strings; the parting comes in a dozen directions; the performer sprawls hopelessly, all thought of his trick departed. . . . Sometimes it arrives like an epidemic. One year six women fell. . . . "I just let go. I couldn't hold any longer." This is the invisible demon of the circus tent. It is always present, working through gravitation, through a headache. Sometimes it comes more into the open; it almost visualizes itself into a personality. (Saturday Evening Post, *December 6, 1930*)

When Ringling Brothers came to town in 1997, I talked to Luis Cabellero of the Flying Caballeros. I had seen him miss the quad in three successive performances and I wondered how that made him feel. He told me, "Some days I feel invincible in the air and other days I don't want to do it. Sometimes you float in the air, you are weightless. Other times you weigh tons and you fall like lead. Sometimes I feel like an angel is holding me and as soon as Ruben [the catcher] appears, the angel lets me go and he catches me."

I have learned to detect the distant early warning signs of the approach of the noon-tide demon. It begins with fantasies of curling up by the fire with a cup of tea, and I find myself singing, "All I want is a room somewhere . . ." Next, I try to pump up my willpower. When this doesn't work and if I persist in my efforts, I make dumb mistakes and lose a few inches of skin from bad landings in the net. Finally it occurs to me that, maybe, it is time to go to ground for a while.

The best thing I can do when I lose my verve is surrender and walk away from the edge for a time. Give up. Stop striving. Do nothing. Enjoy simple pleasures. That is a difficult lesson for an all-American male, because we have had it drilled into us that willpower conquers all. We believe: God helps those who help themselves; when the going gets tough the tough get going; we can do anything we set our minds to—and all the other clichés that are the bread and butter of inspirational speakers. Instead of court jesters, our boardrooms, locker rooms, and professional conventions always have a motivational cheerleader who promotes the magic of willpower. Even genius, we are told, is 10 percent inspiration and 90 percent perspiration.

This is indeed half-true. Clearly, nothing heroic can be accomplished without intention, determination, and willpower.

Alfredo Cadona came to the moment when only an extraordinary commitment offered any promise of a breakthrough. "The long and fatalistic history of the triple deterred me from its accomplishment for years. Then in 1919, I determined either to accomplish it, get killed, or quit trying. So with that out of the way, my mind cleared itself of extraneous matters and exerted itself fully upon the concentration necessary to accomplish the feat. The next spring I went into performance with the triple somersault as a climax of my regular routine.''

It should be equally clear, however, that there are many things that cannot be accomplished by willpower. Friedrich Nietzsche, whose *Will to Power* is one of the great hymns to the kingdom and glory of power, nevertheless let slip the startling observation that ''when politics swallows up all serious concern for real spiritual matters . . . *power makes stupid.*'' This insight, which we are loath to admit, is a humiliating truth. Witness the megastupidities of the twentieth century that were born from the arrogance of power: Hitler's overweening ambitions, Stalin's purge of his greatest generals, the nuclear arms race between the great ''superpowers,'' Pol Pot's ''idealistic'' genocide of the Cambodian people. Have there ever been more stupid wastes of human lives?

It is equally true on a personal level. We fall into great physical and spiritual danger when we attempt to govern our lives by the single ideal of power. Continuous effort exhausts both the body and the spirit. When I try obsessively to accomplish something, and double my efforts with every failure, I eventually discover that some lurking doubt is canceling out my effort. When I must exert an enormous amount of willpower, I come up against a resisting won't-power.

There is a time for conquest and a time for yielding. You have to know when to swim upstream and when to float with the current, when ''to hold them and when to fold them.'' I have to keep constantly alert to resist that most American of all spiritual temptations, the temptation to make ''I can'' into an icon. Sometimes I can't. I cannot will myself to love someone, to have an erection, to go to sleep, to be creative, or to be graceful.

Once I accept my limitations, however, amazing things happen. The other day our troupe was practicing. I was a limp noodle, lackadaisical; no power in my swing, force out, or kick back. My set was low, my break lazy, I let go of the bar too early, and I tucked when I should have opened. Climbing the ladder for another try, I gave myself a pep talk at about the same time I heard my teacher shout, "Do everything with more amplitude. Commit." My next attempt was even worse.

Finally, I took a break and tried to puzzle out what was happening. Allowing my thoughts and feelings to rise into awareness, I realized that a mood of timidity had invaded my entire body. I has a visceral deficiency of courage. My timing was off. My spirit was suffering from jet lag. My mind faxed a clear set of directions but my body was in another time zone. No umph. No verve. No grace.

I had no sooner accepted that it was going to be one of those "no guts no glory" days when I remembered that before leaving the sanctuary of my bed that morning I had a brief dream in which I was practicing the backward somersault to the net—something I had not yet done without safety lines. It occurred to me that, maybe, I should practice falling.

I climbed to the pedestal, grabbed the bar, took off and allowed my swing to die down a little. Then, I kicked forward-back-forward, brought my knees to my chest, tucked and . . . Nothing. I couldn't bring myself to release the bar and fall to the net. Donna, one of my fellow fledgling flyers, volunteered to show me the trick—without the final release. But at the last moment she let go of the bar and completed the trick—her first time. Everybody cheered. I ascended again and went through all the preliminary motions, except this time when the moment for commitment came, I rolled backward, let go of the bar, and landed perfectly in the net. I had done the trick for the first time. More cheers. Next, fifteen-year-old Jaharla decided to try it. She succeeded on her first attempt. And we all cheered. Somehow, we had encouraged each other to do a new thing. We spent the rest of the afternoon falling, again and again, laughing, and being very pleased with ourselves.

There are two morals to this story. The first: if you can't rise to the occasion, you can always practice falling. The second: courage is a by-product of communion rather than an individual virtue, the creation of a compassionate community rather than a psychological quality some people have and others lack.

Blessedly, there are moments when verve and nerve are strong and I rise, effortlessly, to the occasion. For over a year I had been timidly contemplating the rear mount, a move that requires the flyer to return blindly to the pedestal—in a backward position. Time after time, I tried to release my left hand from the safety of the trapeze and make that precarious grasp of the upright that supports the pedestal, which would ensure a safe landing. But I couldn't force myself to do it. With each failure of nerve I badgered myself with a minilecture—"Just do it!"—until I was so discouraged I ceased even to attempt the move to save myself from yet another failure. Then, one day, the wind of the spirit blew from the void and whistled through my bones, and without trying or having to work to overcome inner resistance, I simply did the back mount. And I did it again, and again, until it was securely stashed in my bag of tricks.

The grace factor is the most elusive of the variables that govern my day. Grace, like love, is something into or out of which we sometimes fall. Many of our best moments and creations are accidental, "found art," serendipitous occurrences. I remember a cold, drizzly, February afternoon forty years ago when my mood was grayer than the day and I looked up and saw a red smile on the face of a black woman—a scarlet tanager in the heart of winter—and my spirit soared.

From time to time I enter the zone of grace. Recently I was practicing the plange, catch, and return. Each of my moves was strong, but awkward, as if I had pasted together static postures to form a series. Had you filmed my action it would have appeared jerky like an oldtime movie. Then, suddenly, my body seemed to lengthen and relax. Time became elastic and I broke though some invisible barrier and did three perfect returns from the catcher to the fly bar. "Perfect," I say, not because they were artistically elegant but because they were accomplished skillfully rather than by grit and good luck. I grasped the wrists of the catcher, forced out as we rose to the apex of the arch, kicked back hard during the downswing, waited until we reached the apex of the return arc, pushed, turned in midair and grasped the bar. No! I didn't "grasp" the bar. It appeared and I "accepted" it. Every move just happened; the pieces came together in one harmonious movement and the whole was greater than the sum of the parts.

Unaccountably, there are moments and days when I simply possess an effortless sense of visceral authority. I do not have to exert willpower, so there is no contradictory won't-power, no determination, no set jaw. There is only a total commitment to being in motion. When it happens it is always a surprise.

Moving gracefully, there is no longer any separation between the actor, the act, and the action. The old religious notion of grace refers to times like these when everything comes together effortlessly, and we are whole. In these rare moments when I am myself without having to try, I am at peace with the people I love, with the work that is my vocation, with the place and pleasures I inhabit, with the small tricks I am trying to master.

Grace Happens.

CHAPTER 11

Waiting for the Kairos

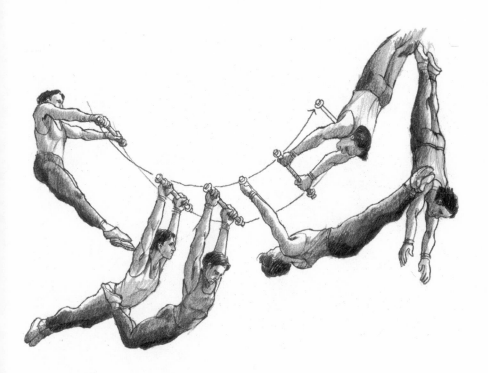

Some days I feel invincible in the air; I float and am weightless.
I feel like an angel is holding me.
Other times I weigh a ton and fall like lead.

Luis Caballero

In the dialectic of the spirited life, no sooner
do we learn one lesson than we are required to learn its opposite. Unto everything there is a time, and a season to everything
under the sun. A time to strive and a time to surrender. A time
to act and a time to wait. The *Tao Te Ching* poses this question
to the one who searches for wisdom: "Who can wait quietly
while the mud settles? Who can remain still until the moment
of action?" Not me. If patient waiting for the right moment for
action is the mark of the sage, my effort to master the straight
jump proves me the fool.

The straight jump to the catcher is a trick that has always
tickled my aesthetic fancy because of its unadorned simplicity.
Pure zen, no frills. The flyer leaves the pedestal, kicks back a
little later than usual, kicks forward, pauses, kick backs, pauses
again, and floats downward to the hands of the catcher.

What makes this trick difficult for the novice flyer is not
the kicks but the pauses. Unlike some tricks in which the flyer
does not see the catcher until the last instant, in the straight
jump the catcher appears in full view early—during the forward kick.

In all of my early efforts I would no sooner see the catcher
within arms length, than I would get anxious, forget the last

back kick, leave the bar, and drop feet downward, forcing him either to dodge or make the catch at a dangerous angle. After rushing, missing the catcher, and tumbling to the net, I was greeted with a mock-serious critique: "You are suffering from PBD."

"What is PBD?" I asked.

"Premature bar departure." And everybody laughed. "Don't leave the bar until the catcher yells "Hep." Wait! Wait! Wait!"

I finally resorted to an old meditative technique of counting. I mentally divided the downhill swing that was to take me to the catcher into five segments and forced myself to count out loud while in motion. I kick back; 2 kick forward; 3 kick back; 4 pause; 5 drop to the catcher. This simple device, like the meditative trick of counting breaths, kept my mind so occupied I had no time to be anxious. When I managed to wait until the right moment for action, I began to complete the straight jump more often than not.

Of course, waiting for the right instant—what the Greek philosophers called the kairos or fertile moment—is exactly what is most difficult for the novice, whether lover, stockbroker, or flyer. Anxiety makes us too eager or too reluctant and forces us to act too early or too late. It is difficult to believe that, at times, as T. S. Eliot said, "The faith, the hope, and the love are all in the waiting."

Alas, the technique of giving my mind something to chew on to distract it from anxiety did nothing to solve my lifelong problem of overanalysis, which became acute in my third year when I began to practice my first big trick—the layout somersault.

The layout marks the rite of passage between the novice

and the intermediate flyer because it depends on the mastery of the fundamentals of trapeze. Although the trick appears simple it is, in fact, very intricate. I had grasped the theory of the layout well enough and had watched enough good flyers accomplish the trick to know what it was supposed to look like. Every practice period I attempted it four or five times and made minor progress in some of the components of the trick. But, no matter how hard I tried to concentrate, my consciousness went into a black hole midway through the trick.

During my 2 A.M. periods of wakefulness, I rehearsed the trick in my mind over and over again. I was certain that if I could just understand each segment I could master it. But my head-tripping didn't work. Like the centipede who walked perfectly until someone asked him how he could keep track of his legs, I suffered from the disease that afflicts the headstrong— the paralysis of analysis. I tried to foresee, plan, and control everything in advance of action. As Zorba said to his friend, "Boss, you think too damn much." The mind-body problem that has haunted Western philosophy since Descartes became a painfully existential dilemma for this philosopher. My body would not do the bidding of my mind. My admirable mental clarity did nothing to free my body to act more gracefully. I was like a man in a prison cell who locked the door from the inside and swallowed the key. I could not *think* of a way to free myself from my mind trip.

I supposed I had thrown the layout a hundred times when someone suggested that I should *visualize* rather than trying to *analyze* and understand it. Preview first; then act. The best concert pianists, track stars, and trapeze artists all seem to practice the great inner game of imagination. So, I sat quietly, closed my eyes, tuned my inner television to the preview channel, and waited. Sure enough, I could see myself taking off, forcing out, setting, breaking and . . . the picture went black. I could see myself making all the moves I had already mastered but couldn't see myself doing something I had not yet done. I tried again. No luck.

After repeated attempts I was forced to conclude that I am not a good visualizer. This is not surprising, since I have never been able to imagine my body making any type of intricate moves in space. I suffer from a mild case of what is, today, called dyslexia. As a child I had a difficult time learning to spell, because I saw the letters of a word in a jumbled sequence. Today, I still reverse numbers and misdial phone calls, one time out of five. Even Arthur Murray's diagrams of dance steps failed to teach me the tango. When I wrestled, the coach would diagram a sequence of holds but I could not understand what he was talking about until I went through the motions on the mat. I can't read a map unless I first face north and turn the map in the same direction. I tried, in vain, to get help by studying videos of great flyers in slow motion, but when I got to the crucial movement I was trying to learn, I could not imagine my way into their bodies. Frustrating.

It was about this time that I received an article from Lisa Hofsess, a professional flyer turned massage therapist:

> *Control in flying is mastered by giving up control. It is one of those perfect Zen meditations in motion. Giving up control is letting my body move with its own ease. My intellectual, analytical mind may know the biomechanics of movement, but it is too slow and calculating to direct it. My mind outlines the basic plan while I am still on the ground, but my body produces the movement in the air.*
>
> *People who watch us . . . imagine we must be out of our minds to do something so dangerous. . . . In a sense, they are correct, because to fly you have to be out of your mind and into your somatic awareness. . . . Without training and highly developed kinesthetic perception and control, it would indeed*

be terrifying and dangerous. . . . To fly, the body must be guided by uninterrupted somatic wisdom. It is the grace of mind-body-emotion cooperation and union.

Flying is crazy if you think about it, but the point is that you don't. You can't think about being in the air while you are there. To be graceful in the air, to fly, you must be in the air. (Lisa Hofsess, "A Somatic View of Flying," in Somatics, *1988)*

Her article showed me the way out of my head and into my body—the path of sensation. I needed to develop my kinesthetic intelligence. I had to abandon concept, analysis, image, and word and go directly to the sensory data that was coming to me from muscles and nerve endings so that I could create an immediate, intuitive awareness of where my body was in space.

The process I invented worked something like this. I would begin each practice session by monitoring signals from my biceps, triceps, rotator cuffs, and so on and creating a muscular inventory that re-minded me of my carnal condition that day. How much umph, verve, and grace might I expect? Following this, each time I stood on the pedestal ready to attempt a trick, I would make sensory contact with my toes, ankles, calves, thighs, hips, and then give them instructions. Concentrating on the sensation from the appropriate part of my body I would say, "Toes be pointed; ankles be together; legs be straight; hips be lithe; body bend like a rawhide whip."

As I began to focus on the sensations rather than the image, I gradually felt my way into my body-in-motion. I still could not visualize the layout but I could feel the slightly sexual sensation of my hips and pelvis thrusting forward as I drove upward, the vertigo as I somersaulted, and the luxurious stretch as I reached toward the catcher.

Daily, this new sense of bottom-up rather than top-down intelligence grows in me and makes it easier for me to trust

what I cannot understand. There is a wisdom in the body—
which is, as biologists say, "a self-organizing system"—that the
mind is reluctant to recognize. I remember the first time, years
ago, when I got an inkling of this notion. I was running at night
on the beach in Del Mar and was worried about cutting my foot
on a shell or piece of glass. I was straining my eyes to try and
see every potential danger. Then, on a whim, I decided to see
what would happen if I ran with my eyes closed. To my astonishment I stepped on fewer potential hazards than when I had
tried to anticipate them. It was as if I had eyes on the bottom of
my feet.

I suspect that the great flyers possess a genius level KIQ—
kinesthetic intelligence quotient—that is as far above the average as Einstein is beyond John Doe. I spent a couple of days
with Tito Gaona at his new trapeze school in Venice, Florida,
and one of the more amazing things he told me was that he
never concentrates on the trick he is doing. As he prepares to
do a triple somersault, he sings or chatters about the meal he is
going to have after the show, or thinks about what he might do
the next day—anything but the trick at hand. "I let my body
do the trick," he says. "It knows how to do it and I don't want
to get in its way by thinking about it."

His brother, Armando, added, "That's why I like it over
on the catcher's trapeze. It is so quiet and peaceful."

I am beginning to see that the goal of practice is not to
learn tricks but to create a new set of instinctual responses, a
second nervous system, a new human nature. From the point of
view of common sense, flying, like radical compassion, is an
unnatural act. Normal people keep their feet on the ground,
their ego boundaries clear, and limit their care to those within
their own family, tribe, or nation. What the practice of trapeze
has in common with the great spiritual disciplines is the hope to
transcend the "normal" limits of the human condition. It requires an unnatural discipline to trust the body to mind itself,

or to trust that we should be compassionate toward strangers and enemies. In both these matters I remain a neophyte.

Notwithstanding my status as a neophyte, ready or not, the big moment arrived. My repeated attempts at the layout had reached comical proportions. I would no sooner mount the board than one of my fellow flyers would announce to all assembled, "And here goes Keen's 172nd attempt at the famous layout somersault." Reluctant virgin that I was, I allowed myself to be persuaded to go for the catch on what we all agreed we would call my 173rd attempt.

As I climbed the ladder to the pedestal, I considered delaying my solo flight, but I knew I would have to confront this anxious moment again and again until I had launched myself into the unknown without any guarantees. Once on the board, I climbed onto the third rise as Tony had instructed me. Someone handed me the trapeze. My hands were sweating and moist in spite of the heavy layer of chalk I put on them. The catcher began his swing and dropped to his knees. I felt the panic rising up through my stomach. What if I break too early, or too late? What if I crash into him? What if . . . ? My mind was racing and the moment of action was rushing toward me at warpspeed. The catcher went into his lock, yelled "Ready," swung toward me, and yelled "Hep."

The moment of truth. The millisecond of decision. I am terrifyingly and wonderfully alone and free.

"H-e-p!" As the force of the final consonant struck my eardrum—the sound of one hand clapping—I lifted the trapeze, jumped to reach it, and launched myself out into the void. All doubt, all thought, fell away and I became a point of focused consciousness. I forced out, swung back, set, broke, threw myself upward, trying to do a handstand on the bar. At the apex I released my hands, looked, and reached for the catcher. And . . . the end of the sentence does not matter. Whether the result was a successful trick is beside the point.

What was created by my decision was my knowledge that I am free to decide.

Most any virtue turns into a vice if carried too far. Supposedly, angels have infinite time and nothing to do except contemplate the glory of God. But for mortals whose days are numbered, time always bears an imprint of urgency that makes waiting and patience virtues only so long as they do not replace action.

My friend Stanley Keleman is fond of saying, "To know yourself you have to sit still, wait, and meditate, but to be yourself you have to act." If you like, chant the great mantra —OM—to remind yourself that you belong to the timeless realm of Being, but be prepared on an instant's notice to intone the other great mantra—HEP—to propel yourself into the timely realm of Becoming.

The results of my 173rd layout were less than poetry in motion. I did not reach that exalted altitude where angels fear to tread. But in my own pedestrian way, I accomplished the first rite of passage. I had, at least, summoned the courage to attempt the big trick.

Chapter 12

Upward Bound

Do you know what it means to fly? To fly is to live. It's the same thing. . . . That's your problem, you're not alive. You have no life and that's not an easy thing to find. First, you must learn to fly. . . . Once you learn how to fly, it's easy.

Brooke Stevens

One fine day, several of our troupe of frequent flyers were talking about how our lives had been changed by our practice. We agreed that the courage we gained in flying had enabled us to take more interesting risks in our professional and private lives, and that our positive addiction to excitement had added zest to everything we did, from sex to cooking.

I began to fantasize out loud about starting a program to offer the experience of flying to two groups of people who I realized could benefit from the courage trapeze affords—troubled teenagers and abused women. I explained I had, thirty years before, worked with Texas Outward Bound to add the "inward bound" dimension to their program. I had no sooner finished sharing my fantasy than two anonymous angels—fellow flyers—offered to give me the money to buy a rig and pay the instructors if I would assume the legal liability and put it on my farm. Both said they didn't want to be openly connected with the project, so the money would come to me in a brown paper bag. "Sounds a little bit like an old-fashioned drug deal," I replied. "But . . . I accept."

My immediate problem was finding out where to buy a trapeze rig. As luck, serendipity, or destiny would have it (all of which have been major factors at each stage of my romance with the trapeze), Stephan Gaudreau had constructed a rig for a client who had then backed out of the agreement, leaving it available for us to purchase.

We erected the rig in the woods in the late fall when the weather was unpredictable, but we had to wait until spring to begin our Upward Bound program. Although I had made contact with several treatment facilities, safe houses for abused women, and programs that deal with "teenagers at risk" during the winter, we did not know exactly what to expect as we awaited our first group of adolescents. We imagined (wrongly, it turned out) that they would be surly kids who would give us a lot of lip and that we might have to deal with anger, resentment, and discipline problems.

The day arrived and a herd of young mustangs galloped and cavorted up the path and milled around the trapeze ground, bumping into each other. A mixed lot of black, brown, and white broncs let free for an outing.

When we got them corralled and calmed down, I assured them there would always be an instructor holding their safety lines and another on the board to help them and that, although they might feel fear, they would be safe. I went on to explain that they could use this adventure on the trapeze as a mirror that would allow them to see how they confront challenges, stress, and fearful situations in other aspects of their lives.

After the warm-up, stretching, and demonstrations, I asked for a volunteer. Several of the boy-men stood up, loudly proclaiming that they were not afraid and announcing that they would rather not use the safety belts, a request we refused. Our first hero mounted the ladder, and we deliberately ignored how he tightened his jaw and exuded bravado to control his shaking. Once on the board he announced, "I'm going to be really good at this," and he followed our instructions and was launched on his flight with no hesitation. After he dropped to the net, he acted very cool and said it was "no big deal," but you could see by his prideful posture that it was a big deal.

His example set the tone for most of the other members of the group. It was as if they were all wearing the "No fear" motto on their T-shirts, and I was reminded of Freud's famous saying, "a negation is the same as an affirmation." If you must announce that you are not afraid, it is because you are. The more timid boys waited until the last possible moment before making their move. A couple of them allowed themselves to be persuaded by group pressure. Two or three had prepared excuses—"I'm not afraid. I just don't want to do it."—"I hurt my back this morning."—"I did this already at the ropes course last year." As we gained more experience with adolescent males, we would find these were typical responses. We seldom encountered "at risk" youth who acknowledged their fear and simply refused to try the trapeze. Fear more often travels with "I can't" or "I don't want to," than "I won't."

When we progressed from swinging to catching, the more athletic members of the group were able to get into a knee hang, and several of them made the trip to the catcher, to the accompaniment of loud cheers. One heavyset girl tried, failed, and announced, "No more."

We urged her to try once more, using our formula. "The first time is for fear; the second time is for fun." The second time, she easily got into the knee-hang position and was very proud of herself. I suggested that she try for a catch, but she protested loudly that she couldn't possibly do that because she was nauseated and had a headache.

"What about fear?" I asked.

"Yea, I am terrified," she admitted.

"Give it one more try and don't try to deny your feeling of terror," I suggested. She agreed, and by the third time she mounted the pedestal, her nausea and headache had disappeared. She swung out, got into the knee hang, reached, and the catcher snagged her—the first female to make a catch. And proud of it.

It was not until the discussion after the session, that the males were willing to talk about fear. "Yeah, I admit I was scared, but I didn't want anyone to know it. I was afraid of what you all would think about me."—"I was so scared I wasn't going to do it, but when I saw my buddies do it, no way I was not going to try it."—"I was scared, but when I saw that you guys weren't going to drop me, I just went ahead and did it."

The most interesting comments centered around getting high. "Man, it was a rush."—"As soon as I overcame my fear enough to jump off the board, I got this rush like I was on drugs, except it was better because my head was clear."—"I have found that natural 'high' I have been searching for, and I am grateful." We shared with them that we considered ourselves "trapeze junkies" and had to have our fix several times a week and joked that we had just given them their first fix, for free. Our session ended with laughter.

As I thought about our adolescent "substance abusers," it occurred to me that our anonymous angels whose gift of money came in the brown paper bag had provided us with an alternative drug. Most premodern tribes created rites, ceremonies, and ordeals that frequently made use of psychotropic drugs to give adolescents an experience of ecstatic self-transcendence. When our society fails to create such ordeals that provide access to the mystical realm beyond the pedestrian reality of nine-to-five, we practically guarantee that there will be a market for those substances that alter consciousness. Humankind cannot live by bread and business alone. We have an instinctual need for self-transcendence and ecstasy.

My experience of the afternoon jogged my memory and I went to my file of ideas and found two items on "ecstasy":

Most experiences of ecstasy are brief and intense. The content of the experience whether triggered by art, nature, sexual love, or religion involves quasi-physical feelings of upward movement, expansion, lightness, renewal, and purification, a sense of a new world, contact with a deeper reality (or God), the extension and loss of the self, a sensation of eternity, a feeling of something limitless, unbounded, something oceanic. (Margharita Laski, Ecstasy)

In principle it is quite easy to make an ecstasy machine. You build, in an empty lot, a high circular fence with a small door. Inside the fence, there is either a deep well that goes down to nowhere or a high ladder that goes up to nowhere. The direction is a matter of taste. Then you let people in a few at a time. . . . Before you let them down into the well or up onto the ladder, you tie a rope around their waist to make sure you can get them back. Since the capacity for ecstasy varies among individuals, as does their height and weight, people can climb down or up as far as they like to find their level of ecstatic satisfaction. This, in essence, is the architectural model of the cathedral, the theater, the lover's couch and the bottle. [And, I may add—the trapeze rig.] (Philip Ennis Jr., "Ecstasy in Everyday Life," Scientific Study of Religion, *Spring 1967)*

In due course, our first group from a shelter for abused women arrived, and we got our first shock. Most had never graced the inside of an exercise facility and were in fair to poor shape. All except one were Hispanic, African American, or Native American, and several had brought babies who were passed around and mothered by everyone. Their initial reaction on seeing the rig was somewhere between awe and disbelief. "No way, sister, am I going to climb that ladder."—"I am scared of high places."—"I am afraid that I can't hold on to the trapeze. I am too weak."

Our first volunteer trembled so much the ladder shook and the only way I could get her to climb further was to accompany her, rung by rung, with my arms encircling her.

Once on the pedestal, she looked as if she had suddenly realized she had made a big mistake. Gamely, she followed our instructions and grasped the bar while the instructor held fast to her safety belt. But when the "Hep" was called, she remained firmly perched on the edge of the platform. Second attempt, same story. Third attempt—liftoff. Out she went into the wild blue yonder, screaming, hooting, and hollering. After a few swings she dropped safely to the net, raised her arms in a victory salute, and did a wobbly dance, on the net.

What followed was a kind of onomatopoeic event with human language imitating the sounds of nature. This particular week, the atmosphere of our trapeze ground was highly charged. A pair of Cooper's hawks had been nesting high in an oak tree above the crane bar that supports the flyer's trapeze. For weeks the young birds cried with excitement every time the parent hawks appeared with a morsel of mouse or other delicacy. Now the fledglings had left the nest and spent much of the day circling the area, playing midair tag, riding the thermals, and swooping down to treetop level, all the while emitting a series of high-pitched screams that blended perfectly with our human screamers. Our women were virtuosos. The ejaculatory screamers let out one big yell of disbelief as they left the platform. The sustained screamers yelled all the way from takeoff to landing. The celebratory screamers began when they dropped from the trapeze to the net, realized they had accomplished the impossible, and emitted a series of exuberant cries: "I-did-it, I-did-it, I-did-it." Each of these individual yells was magnified by the group roar of approval. Occasionally, when there was an interval of silence, we could hear the small cries of an awakened baby.

One after another the women tried their wings. One

woman cried and protested that she couldn't climb up the ladder, couldn't go off the board, all the while she was doing it and looked at herself with disbelief when she completed her flight, as if the whole thing had been done by someone other than herself. When it came time for catching, there were only three or four who were athletic enough to get into the knee-hang position, and of those we only succeeded in making two catches.

In the discussion period that followed when I asked what they had experienced and learned, their comments clustered around three topics—fear, trust, and joy. "I was so scared, I knew I couldn't do it. But when I saw my sisters doing it, I made myself do it."—"I was afraid and I started to panic. Then you made me stop and look around and breathe, and I stopped shaking so hard, and I realized that it is panic—not fear—that has always gotten me in trouble. I was afraid all my life and I used drugs so I wouldn't have to feel it. Then, if I couldn't get my fix, I got in a panic, and I would do anything to get it."—"When I decided I was going to take this risk, and I made myself go off the trapeze, I felt so good about myself."—"I am paranoid. I don't trust people. Especially men. But when you helped me climb the ladder, helped me off the platform, held the safety lines, and caught me, I began to trust you. Now, I see, I have to reevaluate my whole belief that people are always against me."—"I've learned that you can do anything if you put your mind to it, especially when you can trust that you are in safe hands."

Our highest visibility session with the abused women turned out, surprisingly, to be one of the most revelatory. Out of the blue, I received a telephone call from the producer of a documentary that ABC was doing with Sarah Ferguson, the Duchess of York, in which she was to try different adventures—rock climbing, swimming with sharks, a cattle drive. Would we be willing to have her come and participate in one of our trapeze groups with "abused women"? I knew next to nothing about the duchess, but I thought such an event would be fun for the women, and might help our scholarship program, so I agreed to participate.

The grand day arrived. A gaggle of producers, cameramen, lighting experts, miscellaneous grips, best boys, and other mysterious functionaries arrived at our farm with trucks full of cameras, equipment, and food. A motor home for the duchess set up camp in the yard. Hours later, she arrived with hairdresser, security, and assistants whose responsibilities were unclear to me.

I greeted her and introduced her to the women with whom she was to spend the day and was impressed that she immediately committed to memory the name of each person, but I assumed it was a trick that was part of the royal training. What surprised me was the way she proceeded to huddle with and exchange stories with each of the women. By noon the shared stories of trials, sufferings, and efforts to gain self-esteem created an atmosphere of easy banter and mutual encouragement. Clearly, Her Grace had graced the group and become an accepted member—royal but, nevertheless, common.

As the day wore on, and we worked with the women on the skills necessary to get into the knee-hang position and go to the catcher, everyone began to suspect that Sarah was not going to fulfill the expectations of the producers. She was tired, under a lot of pressure, had failed in many attempts, and her hands were hurting. In desperation, we changed the timing of the trick, swinging four times along the arc of the pendulum rather than twice to give her longer to get into the knee hang. This time she did manage to get into the knee hang but too late to make the catch. Figuring that we had only one more chance, we decided to risk the usual timing and hope that she could do it. As she climbed to the pedestal, a hush descended on the trapeze grounds. All eyes and hopes were focused on her. The catcher swung high, went into his lock, and called "Hep" as he reached the top of his arc. She left the board immediately, got into the knee hang, reached, and he got a solid hold on her wrists.

As they swung out and back, the fatigue and tension on her face melted and was replaced by a beautiful glow of triumph. She, like the other fledglings, began to whoop and holler, "I-did-it, I-did-it, I-did-it!" and the assembled multitude broke into applause and surrounded her when she came down off the net.

Later, I asked her what had happened that changed her energy and allowed her to make a catch. "I knew it was my last time, and I figured I had failed, and was going to fail, and the film producer would just have to fix it up somehow. I was tired of trying to please everyone and fulfill everyone's expectations. Everyone tries to control me—the producer, the press, the security, the Palace, everyone. So I just gave up. And, then, it happened."

As darkness descended, the women gathered in a circle to share their experience of the day. A chorus of voices sang a common song: "It is hard for me to trust anyone—especially men."—"I took a risk, faced a fear, and discovered that I was stronger than I thought."—"I was very moved that Sarah paid attention to me and shared her fears and hurts."—"She was one of us."

Sarah spoke last: "I had to trust myself and people I don't know. But I felt the tremendous support of all the women. After making the catch, I had to know the feeling of not being abandoned."

To me it was clear that we had all transcended our individuality and become, for a brief time, a community. I had a strong sense that all the women encouraged and empowered each other. When Sarah made her last attempt, it was as if the will and energy of all the women lifted her to the bar and gave power to her movements. In the end, each person felt not that "I did it" but that "we did it." As one of the women said, "I have been getting in trouble all my life because I wouldn't ask nobody for help. I tried to do it all myself. I couldn't have done what I did today without the support of my sisters."

To hold and enable each other, to fly together and know that "we are" is more fundamental than "I am," is the beginning of the journey from ego to communion.

CHAPTER 13

Becoming a Catcher

In midswing everything turned topsy-turvy. Af-
ter two years of practicing elementary tricks and flights to the
catcher, I began to wonder how things would look from the
other side of the rig. It was time for that great reversal when
the tide begins to flow from the bay back into the ocean, from
the ego into the spirit.

My first challenge was the inch-thick rope that leads up to
the catcher's trapeze. In order to build confidence in flyers and
impress the audience, catchers traditionally climb the rope using only their arms, holding their legs piked at a 90-degree
angle. The very thought of it turned my (otherwise) wiry muscles limp, because I was still haunted by the body image I had of
myself as a scrawny sixteen-year-old in P. S. Dupont High
School. The hero of our gym class, against whom all mortals
were measured and found wanting, was a bantam boy with
bulging biceps who could climb the rope hand over hand. I
could scarcely make it to the top with hands and feet and heavy
cursing. Mentally erasing this imprinted memory, I shinnied
competently up the rope, promising myself that before the year
was out I would make the climb the way the heroes do it.
Look, Coach, no feet!

Once seated on the catch trap, I found it was easy to get it moving by using the kind of body English I had used as a child to pump up the playground swing. It is hard to describe, but like riding a bicycle, if you ever learned it you never forget it. When I had the whole contraption swinging in an arch so high I felt in danger of spilling over the top, it was time to make the next move—getting into the catcher's lock.

In theory, to accomplish this all I had to do was place my hands between my legs, grasp the bar, drop backward to my knees at the front end of the arc, wait until I approached the back end of the arc, and bring my legs out, around the trapeze with the grace of a spider, and entwine them in the ropes. In this way I would be locked in securely so I could hold the weight of the flyer, which I would be unable to do if, as the popular misconception has it, I hung only by my knees.

As usual, fact is more illusive than theory. The first few times, I could not figure out how, when, or where to bend so I could get the balance and leverage to go from a sitting position, backward and down, and come up on the other side of the trapeze with my legs wrapped in the ropes. My rear end stuck out at an angle that kept me too far from the trapeze. After numerous attempts I managed to complete the maneuver in a way that resembled an elephant doing a skin-the-cat.

As you may suspect, this sudden reversal of perspective was disorienting. As a catcher, performing my upside-down, backward ballet, I was supposed to keep my eyes constantly on the opposite end of the rig where the flyer was preparing to make his leap. It was a little like trying to maneuver with a pair of prism glasses that reverse the left and right fields of vision, or trying to shave in a funhouse mirror.

The normal result of this inversion is dizziness and nausea. Many potential catchers are unable to conquer the nausea and are forced to give up. When I was in Las Vegas, Juan Vazquez had described the severe problem he had with nausea at the beginning of his career: "A catcher sits on his trapeze most of the time, with his back to the flyer and he only hangs upside down for a few seconds during each trick. When I began trying to catch my brother I went into my lock and the dizziness hit me. I had to dismount and take a seasickness pill. When I went back up, the dizziness started, but I was determined to push through it. I would muddle through half an hour of practice, hanging for as long as I could while tracking each trick. Then I would have to dismount and sit with my head between my knees to regain my equilibrium.''

Surprisingly, I had no difficulty with dizziness or nausea when hanging and swinging with my head down. At long last I discovered one thing at which I was a natural! A waggish friend suggested I should be a natural catcher because I was already accustomed to philosophical vertigo from looking at things in an upside-down way, reversing appearance and reality, questioning assumptions, and playing with worldviews.

This much at least is true. All my natural liabilities as a flyer proved to be assets as a catcher. My lanky frame, which makes symmetry and precision difficult in turning and tucking, gave me the advantage of a long reach. I could, more or less, telescope myself in or out, which is a useful skill when it comes to adjusting to the differing distances at which a flyer approaches a catcher. My dyslexia, which was a constant source of confusion when I tried to visualize twists and turns of objects and bodies in space, did not come into play when I only had to catch a flyer who was coming straight at me. Best of all, the nagging fear that shadowed my attempts to fly was absent. Catching seemed more of a skill I might learn by persistence than a risk I needed to face with courage.

My next challenge was learning how to build and control the speed and height of a swing as I hung upside down in the catcher's lock.

First, imagine you are hanging upside down and are fused at the waist with the trapeze and your legs are braided into the cable and cannot move. It is now clear that to build a swing and vary its height you will have to use your arms and upper torso in the same way you ordinarily use your legs and hips when you are swinging fully extended from the flyer's trapeze. If you have previously mastered the basic swing and force out and understand the logic of the pendulum, it is not difficult to build and control your swing. To shorten the pendulum and increase your speed, shorten the radius by tucking the body into a ball. To lengthen the pendulum and decrease your speed, lengthen the radius by extending the arms, swimming upward and stalling at the top of the arc. Once I understood these principles and had practiced for a while, I was ready to hang for my first flyer.

My catching guru and I decided to abide by the maxim "Where ignorance is bliss, 'tis folly to be wise," and not inform the novices in the Sunday afternoon beginners class that they were going to fly to a virgin. Better the patient doesn't know it is the surgeon's first operation. Anyway, this wasn't brain surgery and my patients would be tethered to a safety line.

My first catch went so smoothly it was nearly a nonevent. The instructor on the safety lines called the timing, the fledgling flipped smoothly into the knee hang, extended her arms, I grasped her wrists, yelled "Got you," and . . . I became a catcher. I made several more catches that day, and at the end of the class we let them in on our secret. We all congratulated each other, and my first catchee (predictably) said, "I'm glad you didn't tell me. I would have been even more nervous than I was."

Later, there were anxious moments and none more so than when I first caught my teenage daughter, Jessamyn. She occasionally attended a class, so one day I asked if she would fly to me. We looked at each other across the span of fifty years and decided we trusted each other enough to make the attempt.

Once in the catch trap, even though it was a cool day, I noticed my hands were sweating and I gave them an extra dusting of chalk. She took off from the pedestal, swung toward me, and I adjusted my swing slightly so we would reach the catch point at the same time. My arms seemed to reach for her forever as she remained poised in the air across an infinite divide. The moment we grasped wrists the gulf that separates the generations vanished, and we swung out and back together. I knew we had added to the rich harvest of memories that would bind our lives forever into a common story. Of course, I didn't violate the unspoken contract between parent and adolescent and embarrass her by showing how moved I was by the whole thing. There is a time for silence.

Learning the exact science of timing is essential to becoming a catcher. When I began to catch more intricate tricks, my sense of ease and competence evaporated. The difficulty came when I started to call my own timing for the trick rather than depending on the instructor. I seemed to be doing the waltz and the flyer the tango, and the result was cacophony. One of us arrived before or after the beat; we missed each other entirely, only managed to grasp fingertips, or came uncoupled during the dance.

Flyer and catcher swing in their separate arcs, but they must meet at the point where the arcs coincide. As Burt Lancaster tells Tony Curtis in *Trapeze,* as they are attempting to catch the triple, "There is a clock inside you that always knows what time it is. Keep that clock ticking alongside mine." Like two pendulums on a complex grandfather's clock, flyer and catcher must synchronize their movements to the rhythm of the metronome. Otherwise, the moment is lost, and there is no meeting; the pendulum waits for no man or woman.

He and she meet at the apex—tick, swing together out into the apron—tock, swing back toward the empty trapeze that is coming toward them—tick, she catches the trapeze and swings back toward the platform—tock, at the same time he swings alone back toward the apron.

Anyone who has ever struggled with the complex dance of love will have an intuitive understanding of the relationship between flyer and catcher. Keeping in mind that in flying trapeze, unlike lovemaking, you either come together or not at all, there are difficulties of timing and temperament that face all who desire to fly united.

First difficulty. The cables on the flyer's trapeze are usually between eleven and fourteen feet whereas those on the catcher's are eight feet. Thus, he and she swing in different arcs, in different rhythms, in different time zones. The trajectories of our lives vary.

Second difficulty. Flyers come in different heights, from tall to short, and thus add or subtract to the length of the pendulum to which the catcher must adjust.

Third difficulty. Every trick requires a different timing. If a flyer is doing a double layout he will soar higher and remain airborne longer than if he is doing a single layout. The catcher will have to swing lower to allow for the extra time necessary for the flyer to reach the catch point.

Fourth difficulty. The catcher needs to arrive at the catch point slightly later than the flyer, so he is coming from beneath. This way flyer and catcher form a single straight line as they glide downward. If the catch is made at the wrong time, the flyer's body will be at an angle and will whip at the bottom of the swing, doubling the G force and making it difficult for catcher and flyer to hold on to each other.

Since the one constant rule of life is "everything is changing," flying dyads and erotic duos are kept lively, lovely, and lithe by continual adjustment and compromise. Experienced catchers adjust to their partners intuitively. But I, like a nervous novice approaching sex for the first time, have to keep a mental chart of possible positions and timing to consult in midact.

As I go into the catcher's lock, swing out, and glance at my partner on the pedestal, I begin an intricate set of calculations to determine when to call my partner to enter the dance. I don't exactly consult *The Catcher's Primer,* since there is no such text, but these are the rough-and-ready rules of thumb I must keep in mind:

The longer the flyer's pendulum, the more time the trick will take and the sooner I must call the flyer off the board. The pendulum is lengthened by a high swing, somersaults, or a tall flyer.

The shorter the flyer's pendulum, the less time the trick will take and the later I must call the flyer off the board. The pendulum is shortened by a low swing or anything that brings the flyer closer to the bar such as a knee hang, bird's nest, or uprise.

If the timing is too far off, there is nothing either flyer or catcher can do to set it right. It is a problem that also haunts May–December couplings and shadows all love affairs in which partners have different agendas. I was once middle-aged, divorced, and in love with a young woman. We tried to come together but were in different stages of life. I tried to hold her, but she was in the beginning of what I was ending. The day we parted, I sat in my apartment on Telegraph Hill looking out at the city and saw that something strange had happened to the two clocks I could see on the near side of the Ferry Building—they were telling different times.

It is a beautiful thing to fly together. I and Thou—like sun and moon, in separate orbits—join to make one fulsome day.

But to fly, to mate or marry, to care or befriend, we must learn the skills implied by the verbs *adjust, compromise, compensate, attune, harmonize.*

After the science comes the art. Calculation and exactness may be keys to success in the world of Mammon, but bean counters never enter the aerial kingdom.

Flying and coupling both begin with the joining of hands— the sealing of an engagement that was once called "handfasting."

The first of the intangibles in the art of flying, or love, is forging the bond of trust. At the beginning of a relationship, a flyer will naturally wonder if he or she can trust the catcher. Does the catcher know what he's doing? Does he know how to adjust to my rhythms so we won't pass each other in midpassage? Will he make every effort to catch me even if I do an imperfect trick? How much is he willing to risk to make this dance happen? To the degree that a flyer has doubts about the catcher, he or she will have a tendency either to hold back or to grasp, to throw the trick timidly or to try and grab the wrists of the catcher rather than simply trusting the catcher to do the catching.

As the degree of difficulty escalates from a layout to a double, to a triple, to a quad, the flyer must place blind faith in the catcher. As Jill Pages explained to me in Las Vegas, "In the triple and the quad, I never see the catcher. I am spinning so fast and have to open out so quickly that I simply reach and trust he will be there." To accomplish the biggest tricks, I and Thou must make an unconditional commitment to each other.

A catcher earns trust both by his competence and by his willingness to sacrifice his safety to ensure the safety of the flyer. Vilen Golovko, who more than once has been injured when one of the Flying Cranes crashed into him, told me, "I hold the flyer's life in my hands. It is my responsibility to catch him no matter what it costs.''

When I was first breaking in as a catcher, my most willing guinea pigeon was my constant flying companion David Ayers, a man whose enthusiasm and determination sometimes overrides his caution. After catching a couple of knee hangs, we decided it was time to attempt something more difficult that required him to do a high swing and a force out—a back-end plange. I called the ''Hep'' (too late), he forced out, kicked down, and caught me in the forehead with his foot. When I had regained my perch on the catcher's trap, I checked for blood, found none, and called to him, ''Let's try that again.'' And we did, with the same results—another kick in the head. By now our dynamic duet looked like a slapstick act with two stooges, and my face had ugly bruises in a pattern that matched the tread of his shoes.

Once safely on the ground with a bag of ice pressed against my battle wounds, I asked my teacher, ''What did I do wrong?''

''Most everything,'' he replied. ''First, you called the trick late so you were right under him when he was forcing out. Second, you didn't dodge. Third, you didn't protect yourself. You had your arms spread out rather than covering your face. Never open your arms until the last moment when you see that the flyer is coming to you at a safe distance and a safe angle.''

Thus did I learn the first rule of caring and catching. If you don't take care of yourself you won't be able to take care of anyone else. When, five days after my encounter with David, I gave a keynote lecture to the American Association of Pastoral Counselors on domestic violence, I was asked the source of my bruises and black eye. ''I just forgot to duck,'' I replied.

Since I was only semicompetent, the best way I could take care of my flyers was to limit myself to catching those tricks that were within the range of my ability. Without the willingness to sacrifice there can be no flying duets, but there is a limit to self-giving. A catcher must be vigilant and protect himself against the mistakes and miscalculations of his partner. In matters of love, even Jesus advises us, "be as gentle as doves but as wise as serpents."

My second lesson in self-care for catchers wasn't long in coming. David again. This time I called the "Hep" on time, but he hesitated in leaving the pedestal and so arrived late to the catch point. To understand what happened next I need to explain that I was suckled on the Protestant ethic and learned to prove my superiority over lesser denominations of humans by being hardworking, thrifty, and super-responsible. If I am supposed to catch the man, I'll catch him. So, when David arrived late, I extended my body by slipping half out of my lock, stretched to the fullest extent possible, and snagged one wrist and one hand as I was swinging away from him. He whiplashed as we reached the bottom of the arc, which doubled the G force, and I couldn't hold him. He bounced on the ridge rope and ended up in the apron. Since he wasn't dead, and he was David, he jumped up immediately and yelled, "I'm O.K."

In fact, his neck was twisted. After a week, he was still gimpy but game. "I guess we're even now," he said. "I kicked you and you dropped me." I had to remind him that he had kicked me twice.

It took me a while to understand that I had violated one of the most fundamental principles of relationships. Know your limits. If I overextend, under the illusion that I can always save someone who has thrown a bad trick, I double the risk of injury to myself and the other. When someone flies to me crooked, too early, or too late, I need to protect myself, get out of the way, and allow him or her to make a clean fall. Accepting the limits of caring sometimes requires us to let a person fall. One of the hardest things we face with our children and those we love is to allow them to suffer the consequence of their actions. The impulse to help or to rescue at all costs can be dangerous to everyone concerned.

My long experience with marriage has taught me that both parties in any intimate relationship between consenting adults are mutually responsible for the grace or disgrace of the dance that develops.

To the novice, the relationship between flyer and catcher appears unequal. Even among professionals, a lot of playful banter goes on about who is doing what. Tony Steele once asked Slick Valentine, a member of the Flying Valentines, if he could catch his double forward somersault—a catcher's nightmare. Slick yelled back, "You never mind the mule, you just load the wagon." Another time he was throwing the same trick to a catcher who was complaining about it, and Tony told him, "Just close your eyes, hang upside down, and put your hands out. I'll do the rest."

To even as sophisticated a circus lover as Irving Pond, who wrote the classic *Big Top Rhythms,* it appeared that the flyer was inactive once the catch had been made:

> *Without the perfect functioning of the catcher, or carrier, as he is sometimes called, there would be no graceful turn to a catch and no birdlike return to the perch by way of the swinging trapeze . . . for that return depends more upon the strength, accuracy, and judgment of the catcher than upon the agility of the leaper. . . . In this beautiful movement of the return the leaper is not flying . . . but is being hurtled through the air. The catcher has on the instant transformed himself into a human catapult endowed with clear vision, strength, and accurate judgment.*

In fact, the connection is a blend of magic and synergy. As Tito Gaona told me, "There is a mystical connection the moment when you get the wrist-to-wrist connection with your catcher. You can tell whether you should go for the pirouette return or not. It's a psychic connection, a stimulus that goes back and forth at 90 miles per hour. You set the clock to the exact same time. It happens psychically. It's like that with my brother Armando. If I want to do something different, he already knows it. I don't have to tell him.''

The instant before contact is made, the responsibility is all the catcher's. The flyer must "let the catcher do the catching" and refrain from groping and grasping. The synergy begins the instant there is wrist contact when the flyer must respond with an equally vigorous grip, otherwise the inert burden would be too great. I have caught lithe 190-pound flyers who were lighter than leaden 120-pound ones. There was in Hindu philosophy a famous debate about whether God grasps us like a mother cat who holds her kittens by the scruff of the neck or like a monkey who depends on her young to hold to her as tightly as she holds to them. Flying trapeze troupes definitely favor the monkey-grip view of grace. Using the arms of the catcher in the same way as the bar, the flyer forces out at the same time as he is lifted by the catcher to increase the height of their arc as they swing out into the apron. On the return swing the flyer must kick forward, kick back, and push down at the same time as the catcher pushes up. The flyer then turns, not knowing what he will find when he completes his rotation. A third member of the troupe should have caught the bar as it swung back to the pedestal, held it for an instant, and dropped it. But will the return bar be there? Will it be on time? Or will the flyer hear the dread words "No bar," grasp thin air, and fall to the net? Perhaps for the seasoned flyer there is no anxiety, but for the novice, in the instant of making the blind turn toward home, there is a fleeting feeling of dreadful-hopeful anticipation.

In trapeze, as in the moral life, the first rule of responsible action is clarity. "Lucidity is the essence of ethics," Albert Camus said. Be clear about what you intend. When you take aim, there is no guarantee that you will hit the bull's-eye—but you are virtually certain to miss it if you don't aim. But clarity and exactness are never enough. Whether flying or catching, no sooner do I focus, concentrate, and eliminate all distractions than I must relax, allow my eyes to soften, and my vision to broaden. Vilen Golovko described this mind-set to me. "My Aikido master taught me a lot about catching. You have to catch with soft eyes and a soft mind. You have to let go of thinking and go into a meditative state and allow the flyer to come to you."

There are two opposite hazards to avoid—an overtight-narrow-obsessive concentration and an overloose-broad-fuzzy lack of focus. Both are debilitating, no matter what the object of your attention. There is a tyranny of both the CEO and the religious fanatic who concentrate all their attention on a single goal, be it profit or God. Both go too far in the right direction.

The F stop on the camera needs to be able to move back and forth between the extremes. Train your vision to shift from the center to the edges and back again. The eye, like the hand, must learn to tighten and relax, to grasp and to receive. The legendary guru in the movie *Trapeze* advises the young flyer, "Don't leave your fingerprints on the bar." He might also have reminded him that once he flies to the catcher, he should hold to the wrists of the catcher as tightly as he is held. Allow life to come to you, but take hold of it.

The joy of flying is obvious to any spectator watching a flyer soar and spin. The satisfactions of catching are as palpable but are more difficult to discern. The (seemingly) short journey from one end of the rig to the other is a passage through the looking glass to an upside-down world. Becoming a catcher involves a role reversal, a different stance in life, a change in worldview.

The spotlight goes on, the ringmaster announces that the star of the show is about to attempt the big trick—"Tito Gaona will attempt a triple somersault to the hands of the catcher—blindfolded." On the board, Tito's fellow flyers tie the blindfold over his eyes and, for good measure, put a black bag over his head. The audience is hushed, holding its breath. Tito swings, forces out, sets, and drives upward, spinning as he goes. The catcher swings up to meet him; they lock wrists, swing out and back. Tito catches the swinging trapeze and makes a great show of nearly falling as he returns to the platform. The audience explodes in applause. The spotlight again shines on Tito as he styles and bows.

Meanwhile in the semi-obscurity at the other end of the world, the catcher (what is his name?) sits on his trapeze swinging back and forth gently, waiting for the next trick. At the end of the act he will be the first to make his dismount to the net and will take a perfunctory bow. The audience will withhold its accolades for the star.

Everyone understands that, theoretically, the catcher is as important as the flyer, but some deep-seated prejudice keeps us from acknowledging his equality with the star. In our unconscious schema of valuation, the catcher is to the flyer as the lineman is to the quarterback, as the vice president is to the president, as the worker is to the CEO, as brawn is to brains, as matter is to spirit. In the Pantheon of Modernity, fame is reserved for those who dwell on the top of the hierarchy. Service personnel, helpers, caretakers, catchers in the rye or the sky need not apply. From the famous we expect bravado and arrogance; from those who enable them to rise to the pinnacle we expect modesty.

When Tito was the darling of the media, which largely ignored the other family members of the troupe (Richie, Chela, and Armando), a reporter asked his brother and catcher Armando, "Do you get jealous because your brother gets all the attention?"

"No," he replied. "If I want more attention all I have to do is drop him." Catchers, like parents and caregivers, must be willing to be anonymous.

On any normal Tuesday when I am catching, I enjoy a bouquet of quiet peak experiences. More often than not, after I catch fledgling flyers and they drop to the net, they dance around and shout with glee "I did it!" Some few turn around, look up, and say "thank you." I appreciate the recognition that it was *we* who did the trick, but I have already received my reward—the intrinsic satisfaction of catching and the vicarious pleasure of their joy in accomplishment.

To catch someone, especially for the first time, is to share a delight so intense that sexual metaphors come naturally to mind. Here is how Pam Ventura, an amateur flyer who trains with Richie Gaona in Los Angeles, described her experience to me. "I don't know how it is for men, but for most women, your first catcher is like your first sexual experience. A person, usually half-naked, has taken you to some mystical place you've never been before and participated in an aspect of your life that no one else ever has. It doesn't hurt if your first time is at Club Med and the catchers are in their twenties and handsome. Who wouldn't want to throw themselves at some gorgeous, sweaty man in tights who will lift them up to unbearable heights, lead them down the hill like a runaway freight train, and then fling them through the air to a place where they can save themselves by reaching out for something and leave them dangling above the net while people shriek and clap and cheer? Was it good for you? It sure was for me.''

Never underestimate the pleasure of helping.

On my sixty-fourth birthday, after we had been practicing for two hours, my fellow flyers surprised me with an almond cake and champagne. As someone was cutting the cake, I announced that this was going to be an important year for me. Because my father had died at sixty-four, I felt I needed to make some symbolic gesture to announce to myself that a loving son could live beyond the allotted years of his father. ''This year,'' I said, ''I would like to do something that seems impossible. I would like to catch someone's layout somersault and I would like to complete my layout to the catcher.''

My teacher Eric said, ''Climb up in the catch trap and I'll throw you a layout.'' While the champagne lost some of its bubbles and the cake waited, we twice practiced the trick to get our timing right, slapping hands but not making the catch. The third time, we swung out . . . and I made a perfect catch.

In that single moment I shattered a personal and cultural myth about age that had haunted me. At sixty-four I had begun to think of myself and act as if I was getting old. Every day a voice inside of me said, ''You are too old for this. Your muscles, tendons, joints, heart will not stand the strain. It's absurd.'' On the days when my shoulders were sore and my back stiff, I was tempted to believe the voice, hang up my tights, and become a spectator; but when I listen carefully I realize this voice does not originate from my depths. It is the propaganda of ageism that gradually steals away the joy of being and moving and turns us into passive consumers and sedentary spectators. Americans age poorly. Our ideology convinces us to retire from active life at fifty and resign ourselves to becoming brittle of bone, broad of beam, stiff of joint, and short of breath. We convince ourselves that this retreat from vitality is our biologi-cal destiny, the inevitable consequence of aging.

It doesn't need to be this way. Go to the North Beach Park in San Francisco on any sunny day and you will see a hundred or more elderly Chinese men and women practicing tai chi chuan. In the Oriental tradition, age is considered the time of ripening, fruition, and subtle strength. The mind and the spine, like the willow that bends with the wind, should be lithe; the muscles, no longer tensed by ambition and conflict, should move with the fluidity of water that gently overcomes all resis-tance. When the purpose of living is understood as a journey of soul-making, aging is viewed as a process of the fruition of *all* our powers. The body-spirit is to be perfected by time. Even excellence in the practice of the erotic arts is said to be the special gift of the old. The sexual disciplines of Kama Sutra and the Taoist pillow books were designed for those over forty who had gained enough equanimity to cultivate pleasure and soar on the wind without anxiety.

To recite my chronological age is no answer to the question "How old are you?" I am many ages. Any night in dreams I span the range from six to ninety-six. Resting in my father's arms I am once again a child of six; making love with sweet Irene on the sand dunes I am again twenty and overflowing with libido; alone, facing death, I am a withered old man of ninety-six. There are mornings when my body rises up singing and evenings when I am spent and empty of all desire. Nothing seems to age me more suddenly than despair, or return the vernal energy to my body more quickly than hope. When the future seems open, when I realize that I cannot know, predict, or even imagine the limits of the possible, I become ageless. The feeling of being old comes from the sense that our horizons are closing and the best of times are past.

Catching the layout gave me a personal answer to Satchel Page's question "How old would you be if you didn't know how old you were?'' I am old enough to remember that each April I am surprised by lilacs. I am old enough to discipline myself to remain supple in mind and spine, and sanguine of heart. And when I reflect on my strange passion for the trapeze, I can hear the echo of the words of T. S. Eliot:

> *Do not let me hear*
> *Of the wisdom of old men,*
> *but rather of their folly*

A second unforgettable moment in my career as a catcher happened when a masters class we held at our farm with Tito Gaona and Tony Steele was nearing its end. I was tired from a long day of flying and hosting a flock of local trapeze students. Tito and Tony had been throwing tricks to Scott Cameron, our most experienced catcher, when Tito yelled from the pedestal to Aimee Hancock, our one female catcher, ''Well, Aimee, I've never flown to a woman. You want to try it?'' We were all a bit surprised that Tito would risk flying to an unknown catcher, especially since Aimee, for all her strength, was smaller than Tito. Aimee swallowed hard, rolled her eyes in disbelief, and climbed to the catch trap. Their first attempt was just to check their timing, so Tito took off, threw a high layout, and they slapped hands. The second time Tito soared even higher and we all held our breath as he dropped down and they grasped wrists and completed the trick. Aimee, in a state of near Nirvana, descended from the catch trap.

Tito remained on the board and, when the wild cheering died down, shouted, ''O.K. Sam. It's your turn. Are you going to catch me?'' An electric shock went back and forth between the synapses of my brain: Yes-No, excitement-fear, desire-aversion. But how could I refuse such an invitation?

"Sure," I replied with as much cool as I could muster. With my heart pounding I climbed to the catch trap and began pumping up my swing, worried because, even when Tito flies low, he flies higher than anyone I had ever caught.

"Don't worry," he reassured me. "You have great hands. We will just slap hands the first time to make sure our timing is right."

I had no idea of when to call the trick, so I let him call his own time off the board. Out and up he swung into a drive layout so high he seemed to soar into the treetops. When he released the bar he floated downward, slapped hands with me and fell gracefully to the net. Next time, we adjusted the timing slightly. I swung higher, he took off from the board, I followed his trajectory and watched him blast upward. As I swung up to meet him, I pulled my arms to my chest to protect myself until the last moment in case he should come in long and smash into me. As I looked up, I saw him release the trapeze and realized that he was still above the crane bar and had ten feet to fall before we would connect. I extended my arms as he dropped in a swan dive from a frightening height, clapping his hands as he descended. I made a good wrist catch, and we fell downward along the arch of the pendulum. There was a slight jerk as we reached bottom and my spine stretched and crackled because our timing was a bit off. I should have met him closer to the apex so that the fall before the catch would not have been so long. Nevertheless, we held the catch, swung out into the apron together and back, and I released him, and he turned and grasped the trapeze. We both bellowed.

For Tito it required great trust to fly to a novice catcher. For me, it was a journey into a mythic kingdom. For a timeless instant, I inhabited the realm of my own heroes. I was one of the immortals. I had caught the flying man.

CHAPTER 14

The Magical, Mystical Time Machine

Time you old gypsy man,
Will you not stay
Put up your caravan
Just for one day.

Ralph Hodgson

Well into my fifth year of practice, lots of strange things were happening—distortions in my sense of time, "psychedelic" or "mystical" moments in which I suddenly found myself elsewhere. Without warning, I slipped through wormholes in the time-space continuum, flew through invisible boundaries between time and eternity.

As the result of these weird experiences, I began to think of the trapeze rig not so much as a school for wisdom as a machine for time travel, not unlike those contraptions in old movies constructed by mad scientists in their garages. On any ordinary day when I climbed inside its spindly superstructure of aluminum pipe and nylon rope, I might be launched on a voyage into an unexpected mode of time. As I grasped the trapeze and left the pedestal, I could never be certain whether I would remain focused in the present moment, travel backward, forward, or sideways in time, or transcend all sense of being in time. For all I knew, time might speed up, slow down, or stop altogether.

It all began with my battle with the Speed Demon.

The day after the masters class I was practicing face-offs to the net—an elementary fall in which I release the trapeze when

I am parallel to the net in a face-down position, do a half-turn in midair, and land on my back. Each time I tried, I started turning before I had even released my hands from the bar, because I was afraid I wouldn't have enough time to turn before hitting the net.

Tony Steele, who hadn't yet returned home to Reno, was watching my frantic efforts and yelled at me, "Sam, you have plenty of time. Don't hurry. Float down halfway before you begin your turn."

My immediate response was, "Tony, *you* may have plenty of time, but *I* don't."

He laughed, and then he climbed up to the pedestal to demonstrate. Whereas I plummeted like lead, he glided downward like a feather on the wind. His movements were so relaxed as to appear almost languid, and he seemed to have twice as much air time as I did.

Watching him, I understood that his movements are leisurely and fluid because he has an inner sense of the spaciousness of time. He perceives in slow motion; his inner clock runs at half-speed. By contrast, I have an inner sense of things happening so rapidly that I have no time to react. My mental clock runs at double speed. Anxiety about not having enough time causes me to speed up my pace to the point that I am actually moving too fast and my movements become jerky and uncoordinated, like Charlie Chaplin in the old silent films.

Like most modern successful men and women, I have inadvertently become a slave to the Speed Demon. I suffer from that diseased sense of time that infects those who live in the fast lane—Type A achievers, men and women on the go. Almost all of us who are bedazzled by the promise of prosperity and happiness through the market economy have become adrenaline junkies, chronically stressed and distracted by trying to do too much too fast. Hurry up. To the speedy belong the spoils. FedEx it, get it there tomorrow. If that is too slow, use e-mail.

Speed up your brain and your nervous system or else you will fall behind.

The velocity necessary for success exceeds the rate of reflection. The faster events move, the faster we move to try to keep up with them until we are overwhelmed by the escalating pace. In managing a business, as in learning to fly, the problem is especially severe. Any trick in the competitive marketplace, or midair, is a series of millisecond moves, each of which must be done on time and in the right sequence in order to succeed. The Speed Demon has created the illusion that we must spin at sixty miles per hour to achieve success. We suffer from the illusion that the faster we run the more likely we are to grasp happiness.

A famous incident in the history of trapeze illuminates the myth of speed. Alfredo Cadona, the first flyer to perform consistent triple somersaults, described this trick in a way that is an apt metaphor for the dilemmas all of us face who live in the ever increasing velocity of what we call "the modern world":

> The history of the triple somersault is a history of death. . . .
> The struggle to master it has lasted more than a century . . .
> and has killed more persons than all other dangerous circus
> acts combined. . . . The reason lies in the terrific speed. . . .
> At a propulsion of more than sixty miles an hour the space
> gauges of the brain have ceased to function properly and for a
> split instant one loses all knowledge of time, space, distance,
> or surroundings. . . . The success of the triple lies principally
> in the reestablishment of brain coordination. For an instant I
> spin as though I had been caught in a whirlwind and then my
> brain begins to fight for renewed control. It is comparable to a
> swift recovery from unconsciousness. The tent, the music, the
> roll of the band's drumbeat; hearing, sight, sense of direction,
> knowledge of surroundings—all have been instantaneously
> absent. Then, suddenly, I am alive again. I am falling and

spinning as I fall. The sudden deadness of my brain is jerked instantaneously to life. From far away a vague, filmy mirage rushes toward me with the speed of a bullet—the eyes, growing swiftly larger and more luminous. . . . Suddenly the eyes lose their grotesqueness; they become humorously lighted, normal eyes of my brother, Lalo. I feel the grip of his strong fingers upon the silken taping of my arms; my own hands grip his taped wrists; I hear the applause of the audience; I am swinging safely beneath his trapeze (Saturday Evening Post, December 6, 1930).

For years, Cadona's description of his experience was an unquestioned dogma that bedeviled trapeze performers. Flyers trying to learn the triple expected to suffer speed-induced brain lag and to be disoriented. Consequently, they were. The uncritical press promoted the myth and upped the ante by proclaiming that when Miguel Vazquez completed the first quadruple somersault he reached the speed of between seventy-five and eighty miles per hour.

The problem with the long-accepted accounts of the speed necessary to accomplish "the big trick" and "the biggest trick" is that they are absurdly wrong. Harry Graham—the author of Tito Gaona's story, *Born to Fly,* and Miguel Vazquez's story, *The Biggest Trick,* and a personal friend of both flyers— heard the cliché so often he decided to apply a little math and physics and check it out. He concluded that neither speed was physically possible. "A mass travels sixteen feet during the first second of free fall, forty-eight feet during the second, and eighty feet during the third second" (*The Biggest Trick,* p. 188). Since Miguel was airborne for only 1.6 seconds before reaching the hands of the catcher, his actual speed was about seventeen and a half miles per hour. For him to reach a speed of seventy-five miles per hour, it would take about 3.4 seconds and a fall of 190 feet.

Further to the point, many professional flyers have assured me they experience none of the brain lag that Cadona reported. Stephan Gaudreau says he has a leisurely feeling when he throws the triple and never loses awareness of his position in space. Recently, I was watching Sergei Beloujenkov of the Flying Cranes practice the quintuple somersault. He spun with such breathtaking speed and opened so rapidly to reach the hands of the catcher that I assumed he must suffer from horrible vertigo, but when I asked him about it, he said in a matter-of-fact way, "No, I always know just where I am at any moment when I am in midair."

Here was my dilemma. Master flyers may have a sense of leisure, but for fledgling flyers Cadona's description of the distorting effect of rapidity is accurate, if not understated. How could I go about transforming my inner sense of time so that I might feel leisurely even when I must move rapidly?

I knew a few little tricks that were helpful. I could confront my anxiety about not having enough time and make a conscious effort to slow down. Before I started a trick, I forced myself to breathe deeply and slowly and reminded myself not to hurry. These things helped, but they were not enough. Something about my experience and philosophy of time needed to change before I could remain still and mindful while living in the eye of the hurricane.

The change in my philosophy of time was triggered by my experience of the eternal moment at the place called Top.

During my first years of practice I was an untimely mess, a dancer with two left feet and no sense of rhythm. I tried hard enough but just couldn't get the right timing for anything. My force out was awkward, my break weak, my kicks untimely; my flights to the catcher always left the gate either too early or too late. My basic problem was that I lacked an unchanging reference point by which I could judge where I was in the trajectory of the pendulum. Typically, my teacher would say, "Don't initiate your back kick until five feet before Top, or don't release the bar until you are at the Top."

The place called Top is true north on the flyer's and catcher's compass. Until you learn how to find it, you are bound to get lost because all action is initiated in relation to this mystical point. It is easy enough to understand where on the map Top is located. At the apex of every swing, between the rising and the falling, there is a point of absolute stillness where the flyer is weightless.

You would think that finding Top would be as easy as breathing. Well, it is as easy—and as difficult. Since the unique dignity of human beings is connected to our capacity for leisure, wonder, and contemplation, the practice of stillness should come naturally to us. Anyone should be able to follow the wisdom placarded on every railroad crossing—Stop, Look, and Listen—but everything encourages us to race the train.

It turns out, as Lisa Hofsess explains, that "most flyers continue to miscalculate the peak long after they have lost their fear of being on the trapeze. Even experienced flyers have to concentrate on finding the still point in each new trick. The peak changes with the height of the swing; it is perceived differently in each of the many positions on the bar from which tricks originate, e.g. upside down, facing forward or backward, hanging by the hands or knees, or balanced on the hips" (Lisa Hofsess, "A Somatic View of Flying," in *Somatics,* 1988).

Great dancers, gymnasts, and flyers have an instinct for rhythm and timing. By keeping their motion sensors attuned to the still point, they know the difference between the time for effort and the time for relaxation, the time to close and the time to open, the time to hold tight and the time to surrender.

At any moment they can orient themselves in midair by finding the still point in the dance.

I, on the other hand, am rhythmically challenged, just as I am deficient in the cat gene that controls the instinct for safe landings. In my chaotic swinging along the pendulum of time, I tried to get a reference point by keeping my eyes set on a stationary mark, in this case the crane bars. If only I could find an absolute unmoving object in the flux of time I could locate Top. The stillness, the surcease from movement, always escaped me. All my life I have been striving for peace, searching for a place to come to rest.

One day after I missed two catches because my timing was off, my flying master shared a bit of the esoteric lore that is entrusted only to the initiated. "Take a few practice swings with your eyes shut and listen to wind in your ears. When it stops you are at Top," he said.

It didn't seem to me that I had enough spiritual potency or earthly power to create a wind. But when I tried it—sure enough I did. Out I swung to the accompaniment of whoosh, and back to whoosh, and between the whooshes of the wind there was the silence of the void. Instantly, in what must have been a minisatori, I arrived at Top and knew it as a place I had been many times before but had never recognized.

Christie Shipp, a fellow frequent flyer, has her own unique method of locating Top. "When I fly I pull my hair back in a ponytail, but I leave a few wisps of hair free to flutter in the wind created by the swinging motion. This is my personal windsock that indicates my speed and direction. When my hair stands still I know I am at Top."

It is as the old Zen masters said in their teachings about breath and enlightenment: "As breath turns from down to up, and again as breath curves from up to down—through both these turns, realize. Or whenever in-breath and out-breath fuse, at this instance touch the energy-less energy-filled center.

When in worldly activity, keep attentive between the two breaths, and so practicing, in a few days be born anew" *(Zen Flesh, Zen Bones,* Paul Reps, p. 269).

If I could remain for the flickering of a moment in the zone between inspiration and expiration, between the uprising and the downfalling, between effort and rest, I might catch a glimpse of the place where gravity and grace meet. Once I discovered this stillness I could move in a leisurely way.

The significance of what the animal in me—or should I call it my soul?—learned in an intuitive way about Top did not register until Vilen Golovko, of the Flying Cranes, put it into words. Taking a napkin, he drew the eternity sign—a figure eight lying on its side. "The idea of flying is connected to the idea of eternity," he explained. "The pattern etched in space by a flyer doing a simple swing and force out coincides with the eternity symbol. The flyer takes off from the pedestal, drops down, swoops up in the force out, goes around the curve, crosses through the middle, kicks back and rises to the top of the arc to complete the figure. Twice in the journey he reaches points of absolute stillness."

When my experience of Top came together with the eternity symbol, the penny dropped, the key and the lock came together—or, as they say these days, I experienced a paradigm shift. In a flash I understood in my gut that eternity is present in every moment, if only I know how to locate it.

As I thought more about it, some of the mystics I had studied in my days in theological school and had failed to understand began to make sense to me. All existing things, every atom and Eve, inhabit that paradoxical realm beyond rational understanding that T. S. Eliot called "the still point of the turning world." We live in the eighth day of creation in which Being is always Becoming. Like cosmic gypsies, we dwell in an ever receding instant poised between a past that is no longer and a future that is yet to be. To speak authentically, to live soulfully, to fly gracefully, we must continually travel back and forth across the frontier between silence and words, stillness and action, the Top and the trick.

From my experience of Top, I gained a measure of understanding of what the hymns I sang as a child were all about.

> God of our life, through all the circling years
> We trust in Thee
> God of our past, our times are in Thy hand;
> With us abide.

It seems to me, the word *God* in its most profound usage refers to our experience that our brief moment in time is encompassed by something that is not subject to the logic of time. "God" is the imagined perspective created when the experience of timelessness gives us the certainty that our linear sense of time is, ultimately, an illusion. "God" is the way the religious imagination articulates the awareness that time is not running out, and there is no need to hurry.

Further to the point, my ordinary daily life began to be interrupted frequently by mystical moments in which time evaporated and left behind only the events that were happening. It is almost impossible to describe such experiences because they have no extraordinary content. It is not that something miraculous is added to the landscape, but that something is subtracted. For instance. One morning I was sitting at my desk going about the routine of making phone calls, answering letters, and trying to clear away the clutter so I could get to my writing. My attention was interrupted by a yellow warbler that was sitting on a branch outside my window chatting up its mate in a nearby tree, to the antiphonal sound of the low gurgling of the creek. Suddenly, time—that "like an ever rolling stream, bears all its sons away''—vanished and there was only Being. I, who am usually self-conscious and caught in the urgency of doing, came to absolute rest and was transported into the timeless realm of Presence where I was no more or less important than a bird and a brook. How can I say it? I inhaled the bird anthem and water music and became a slow and deep breathing. I ceased to be a human doing and became a human happening within a myriad of other happenings, a being within Being. I suppose that the mystical moment, by clock time, lasted only a few seconds, but it was enough to give me a vacation from the urgency of time, fill me with a sense of gratitude, and change the rhythm of my day.

The more I dwell in stillness for brief moments in my flight through time, the more I know in my gut that the secular—clockwork—version of linear time as measurable units is a Procrustean bed for my spirit. The clock and calendar measure movement without meaning, flux without purpose, change without direction, only velocity driven by anxiety over scarcity and death.

The experience of eternity, no matter how brief its duration, provides me with the antidote for the disease caused by the Speed Demon. The feeling of being at Top attunes me to a different cadence, resets all my interior clocks, inserts a sense of leisure into the rhythm of my breath, blood, and mind. It seems ridiculous to say, because the scales show no difference in my weight, but I swear I have lost ten pounds since I experienced Top. It feels as if there has been a metaphysical shift in the structure of the atoms that make up my body-mind-spirit.

I began to suspect that the great mystics and flyers discovered a fundamental natural law of the universe as important as, but opposite to, the law of gravity—*the law of levity*. From the perspective of the spaceless-space and timeless-time at Top, ''reality'' and ''appearance'' switch places. Newton's apple flies from the ground back up to the tree. Everything that falls rises again, and everything that dies will be resurrected. If astronomers and cosmologists had eyes to see they might discover that beyond the black holes in space there are white wholes in time in which new worlds are constantly being created. In the ultimate scheme of things, the second law of thermodynamics is revoked; destruction is seen as only a moment within the life of creation. There is no other way to explain how heavy atoms can be assembled into an indigo bunting, or how a flyer can spin a quintuple somersault, or why, upon occasions, I now float on air.

Simone Weil, the French philosopher, would-be saint, and explorer of gravity and grace, was well acquainted with the kingdom of the airborne even though she was never on a trapeze:

> *Man escapes from the laws of this world but only for the space of a flash of lightning. Moments of pause, of contemplation, of pure intuition, of mental void, of acceptance of the moral void. It is through such moments that he is able to approach the supernatural. . . . Whoever for an instant can endure the void either receives the supernatural bread or else falls. Terrible risk; but we have got to run it. (Simone Weil,* Notebooks*)*

My fellow trapeze enthusiast David Katzenstein, the CEO of a large corporation, is a remarkable flyer who lacks the fingers on his left hand but is able to pinch the bar with his thumb. He gave voice to a feeling that is common but usually unspoken among flyers. "I keep trying to understand why I am so captivated by the mystique of the trapeze. Most of my life is on the horizontal dimension. I have been running a large company for twenty-five years and I get wound tight as a spring. But the moment I climb to the platform and take a swing, I get a wonderful sense of inner peace. The brief seconds of flying are *an explosion into the vertical dimension* during which I experience the silence of my spirit. Some people talk about getting an adrenaline rush, but it is exactly the opposite for me. I get a silly grin on my face and a glow that has nothing to do with physical exercise. I think the trapeze allows me to let my spirit feel as it is supposed to feel—to soar, to be unfettered, to be unbounded."

We dream of flying because we are never satisfied for long with life on the horizontal plane. Something we call "spirit," for lack of a better word, impels us to become explorers of the vertical dimension.

In our time, the religious and metaphysical hierarchy—the great chain of Being, with God at the apex, the Devil in the pit, and the space between inhabited by angels, humans, animals, and demons—that was the foundational vision of Western civilization is in danger of being replaced by the one-dimensional promises of the market economy. The developed and developing world has become a monotone landscape where the masses long for Coke, McDonald's, and Sony. Advertising, the pornography of the market economy with its promise that we will be satisfied by the latest gadget, is a horizontal-secular sublimation of our vertical-spiritual impulse. Our yearning to fly is being twisted into an obsession to consume.

Commonly, the uninitiated confuse flying trapeze and skywalking or high-wire performance. When I tell someone I practice trapeze I often get the response, "Oh, like the Great Wallendas." The Wallendas were at one time the most famous and daring high-wire *walkers* in the world. If they were flying, it was very bad news!

The tightrope has, not surprisingly, become a favorite metaphor of American business. CEOs, especially, like to think that theirs is a life on the high wire: they walk a very thin line between point A and point B, must keep their balance, and (supposedly) work without a safety net. The precarious journey of the solitary high-wire walker may be a fitting metaphor for a one-dimensional secular worldview. So long as we do not transcend the horizonal dimension, we remain pedestrians on a perilous journey over the abyss without the possibility of an "explosion into the vertical," or "everlasting arms" waiting to catch us.

Stopping time (for just an instant) is different from either slowing it down or transcending it altogether.

Many athletes get an inkling of the law of levity and some few learn the esoteric skill of making time stand still. At first, it usually happens in the middle of a highly charged game purely "by accident" (a sloppy category that begs the questions of cause and meaning). Perhaps the excitement is already stirring the atoms into a frenzy. It is the closing seconds of the game. The quarterback throws the ball—too high. The wide receiver jumps and will, obviously, miss it. Then, suddenly, something strange happens—time stands still. Against all odds, the receiver continues to ascend and catches the ball. Should you ask him after the game how he managed to make such a miraculous catch, chances are he would say something like, "I don't know. I saw the ball and knew I couldn't reach it, and then it was as if time stopped, and I kept soaring upward and the ball appeared in my hands."

Time usually moves in an orderly fashion. The seconds follow each other, sixty to the minute. The camera filming the event, like the rational mind, shows only continuity of action. One thing leads to another, and another and another, in a perfect chain of cause and effect. Then, in the middle of time *(chronos)* there is a special moment *(kairos)* when sequential time stops. Unaccountably, an instant is freeze-framed; then the film rolls again at full speed.

The first time it happened to me, I was throwing a reverse knee hang to the catcher. In this trick, the flyer approaches the catch trap backward and at the last moment drops into the knee hang and grasps a bar that is held by the catcher. Everything was proceeding normally and I was a millisecond from completing the catch when I saw that the catcher was only holding the bar with one hand. Immediately, I freeze-framed the instant and all action stopped while I examined the picture. It seemed as if I spent a long time considering the question: What's wrong with this picture? before I pulled myself back up to the bar and aborted the trick.

During these special moments an athlete enters a mini white whole in time where impossible things become possible because the law of gravity is suspended. Like certain saints who were reputed to levitate, many athletes seem upon occasion to become weightless. The widow of the great dancer Nijinsky said he took a leap, held his breath and stayed up, felt supported and could control his descent. Mikhail Baryshnikov was said to have had a balloon that allowed him to ascend into the air, defy gravity, and revolve two full turns before landing. Michael Jordan regularly soars higher and stays suspended longer than is natural for an earthbound man.

When I asked Miguel Vazquez to explain how he did the quadruple somersault, he said, "In the quad you lift up your legs and it feels like something is pulling you. Your body carries you to a different height. . . . I can't really explain it. . . . I go up with a lot of power, reach a peak, and then I feel like I stay in one place for a long time. If you look at the video, it shows me staying in one place and spinning. You don't learn this feeling; it comes naturally. I couldn't tell you how to learn it."

In my sixth year of practice as I am getting more at home in the air, I am discovering something about the experience of time that none of the textbooks of philosophy or psychology told me.

Fear is an accelerator. It speeds time up, makes me move in a frantic way so I do not miss . . . the trick, the money, the gusto. The sense of urgency, of not having enough time, that sometimes dominates my trapeze practice as well as my daily life is created by a complex of unconscious fears.

In the degree that I am governed by fear I become breathless and rush everything. I think about the next move rather than remaining in the experience of the moment. This is particularly crippling when I am trying to do a layout and I start thinking about making the catch before I have finished the trick. Or in lovemaking when I become anxious about reaching the "goal" rather than enjoying the journey.

Boredom, by contrast, is a brake that slows time down to a deadly pace. There are times when meaning and excitement vanish from my life. I am not engaged; I am bored, and an endless series of leaden moments seems to stretch out before me like bad eternity. I have too little energy, verve, or imagination and cannot bring myself to act. Time is both empty and heavy on my hands.

What I am beginning to think of as the essential religious sense of time is radically opposed to either fear or boredom. The experience of transcending time at Top, or slowing it down, leads to a sense that the moment is sufficient unto itself, that time is passing neither too fast nor too slow and that I may, therefore, be leisurely. Someone translated the Old Testament saying: "Be still and know that I am God" as "Be leisurely and know that I am God." Whatever it is that allows us to inhabit time in a leisurely way, to trust that we may give ourselves to the present moment because something of abiding value is unfolding in the process of our becoming is a sacred reality that might well be called "God" or the ground of our Being.

On rare occasions, I climb to the pedestal and I forget to be anxious. Perhaps I am too exhausted to be afraid, but in those times I seem to be almost a spectator of my own action. Peacefuly, I wait for the pregnant moment in the middle of acting; I wait for the fruit of my practice to drop from the tree by itself; I wait for my doing to arise effortlessly from my being. And, the trick I have struggled to perfect simply does itself. Refreshing.

These strange experiences of transcending time or stopping it for a moment continue to puzzle me. They throw my Ivy League educated mind into a dither, but they inoculate me against the disease of clockwork time.

It is only in modern cultures that men and women have surrendered to the tyranny of the clock and made a virtue of a frantic pace of life and metaphysical despair. Look at the inside page of the *New York Times* and you will see the icons of our secular minds. Our great emblem of the successful life is the extravagant watch—Rolex, Piaget—that tells the seconds, minutes, hours, months, phases of the moon, but not when or where or whether time intersects eternity. The secular world knows time as the battlefield on which the struggle for success is fought. Time is money and money makes the world go round. Time is running out. You only go around once, so you'd better make efficient use of every minute, grab the gusto. Time is of the essence and can be saved by going faster. For fourteen thousand dollars the diamond-encrusted Piaget tells us only the affluent time of *homo economicus,* the economic animal. It knows nothing of the seasonal time that governs the life of the Bhutanese villager, nor the quantum point where time ceases as it approaches the speed of light.

If all I hear with the ear of my spirit is the incessant sound of the clock, tick, tock, tick, tock, tick, tock, my awareness of passing time creates an existential agony. The pendulum of the old grandfather clock is ruthless, the march of time inexorable.

The moments of my days are numbered. The clock marks the seconds, minutes, hours that bring me to the end of time. Finis. Death. All my instants add up to oblivion. How can I rest easy and be at home in time when it carries me inevitably toward death and oblivion?

The experience of abiding for an eternal instant at Top puts me in touch with that dimension of my being I call "spirit" or "imagination" that refuses to accept death as my final horizon. Without giving me any notion of my ultimate destination, it suggests that my destiny is to be a time traveler and not a clock watcher. If I live by the clock, I will die by the clock. When I claim my own time and space I am able to fly through my days with the greatest of ease.

There are other distortions that happen to those who enter the magical, mystical time machine, which I feel obliged to report—even though it makes me feel rather like a tough-minded journalist who, not believing in ghosts, begins to experience unexplained presences and occult happenings in a haunted house.

Under the influence of Dionysius in 1969, I took a sabbatical leave (from which I never returned), traveled to California, and fell under the influence of the Zen–Gestalt–New Age gospel. Like Jack Kerouac, Timothy Leary, Ram Dass, Fritz Perls, I wanted to live in the moment. Be here now. Just do it. Go with the flow, forget the past, stop worrying about the future. Dutifully, I took the psychedelic wafer, inhaled the sacred smoke, and practiced sensory awareness. I sat cross-legged, counted breaths, and meditated.

By and large, I was no more successful at being a secular saint than I had been at the Presbyterian equivalent. I was a failure at living exclusively in the present tense. Blissful as it was to inhabit an ego-less moment of awareness or action, my past and future kept coming back like a song. Carlos Castañeda warned me that I would never become a warrior unless I "erased my personal history," but I cherish my memories of childhood and enjoy the photograph albums that contain the chronicles of my years. Nor was I willing to extinguish my dreams of one day living on a ranch on the trailing edge of some great mountain. It seemed to me then, as it does now, it would be terrible to have no remembrance of things past or hopes for things to come.

During my first couple of years of trapeze practice, I often experienced the state of abiding in the here and now that had eluded me in formal meditation. One of the most predictable joys of flying (once fear is domesticated) comes from the experience of being absorbed in the present moment. The catcher calls "Hep"; I step off the pedestal and (I) disappear. There is only swinging, forcing out, sweeping, and throwing the trick to the waiting hands of the catcher. All verbs, no noun. All action, no self-consciousness. The trick begins, my ego goes on vacation, (I) disappear into a focused point of awareness and am blissfully forgetful of both myself and the passage of time. I do not think about the rent or the millennium.

When I look more closely at the experience of "the present moment," however, it is never so pure as it initially appears. If I unravel the strands very carefully I find that the braid of present experience contains a rich collage of images, scenes, and feelings flowing toward me from both the past and the future.

On almost any afternoon when I am practicing by myself and the stream is gurgling, the alchemy happens. The trapeze bar becomes a grapevine and I slip back across a half-century of years into the College Woods and feel the luxurious freedom of an endless summer afternoon stretching before me with nothing to do except hunt for crawfish in the creek or watch a wood thrush feeding her young. "Backward, turn backward, O Time,

in your flight / Make me a child again, just for to-night!''
(Elizabeth Akers Allen) It is easy to say, I am just remembering.
But, I don't have some black-and-white photographic image of
my "inner child" superimposed on the Technicolor experience
of the present. I *am* once again the boy swinging on the vine.

Alfredo Cadona reported a similar experience of finding
the past suddenly intruding into the present and called it
"sideslipping." It both intrigued and disturbed him because he
thought of it as a mental disturbance.

> *Sometimes . . . the strangest of all mental disturbances occurs.*
> *Somewhere in the intricacies of the trick, my brain has side-*
> *slipped, and as I fall to the net, it continues its vagaries.*
> *During that instantaneous drop I may be out fishing, or*
> *walking along Fifth Avenue in New York. . . . I see friends I*
> *have not met in years that I have otherwise forgotten. I look*
> *down upon my father, standing in his practice clothes in the*
> *building at Shreveport, and shouting directions to me.* (Satur-
> day Evening Post, *December 6, 1930*)

Tito Gaona told me of an even more radical experience of
porous boundaries between past, present, and future that happened to him. One day he was performing in a circus in Los
Angeles and went out for a run. Without any knowledge of his
whereabouts, he jogged into a cemetery and found himself
standing in front of the sculpture of the winged angel that
marks Alfredo Cadona's grave. From that time on, he began to
feel Cadona's presence. "When I was at the Monte Carlo Festival I was very nervous. When I got up on the board I felt a pat
on the back and I heard Cadona say "It's yours, kid." And I
flew like I never flew in my life. When I came back to the board
I did it just like Cadona—I looked down. . . . My style is to
look up. I looked at the videotape and it's there. I feel that
Cadona is my angel; he is protecting me. One time in Switzer-
land, the spreader on the net broke and I was flying out of the

net. At the last moment, something was there to help me—Cadona. A cable caught on my back and threw me against Armando's rope-catcher's ladder and I was saved from serious injury. It is almost like I am possessed by his spirit. I think I am here to complete what Cadona didn't complete in his life."

It is as if the arrow of time ceases its forward motion, does a boomerang back into the past, and then continues its flight toward the future; or, as if, time is a pedestrian walking down a narrow road who suddenly decides to throw a backward somersault.

These metaphors are too simple to capture the complicated tricks time has up its sleeve. It also performs a forward somersault in which the future flips into the middle of the present.

A lot of flyers report a kind of precognition. Jill Pages, told me about the first time she caught the quad: "One night I was practicing, I thought about my mother and I wanted to do something to express my appreciation to her. I thought: I'm going to do the quad tonight. I was taking a break, lying on the board, and I went into a zone—way out. I felt like I was in the stars. I don't know how long it was. It seemed like a long time. It was wonderful. I prayed, and lay there and relaxed, and felt and imagined what it would be like, and it was done. If I was going to do the quad, I was going to do it that night. I did it on the sixth attempt."

The same thing happened to me when I was working on learning to return from the catcher to the trapeze. After many failed attempts, I had exhausted both my reservoir of energy and my willpower. I was ready to give up for the day, but the precise moment I took the fly bar in my hand to swing and drop to the net, my eyes fell on the spiral pattern of the tape wrapping and I "saw" myself having already accomplished the return. I yelled to the catcher, "One more time." And, it happened in fact just as I had seen it in my mind's eye a moment before.

An analogy taken from biology gives me a tentative intellectual handle on the puzzling past-present and the future-present character of time. Biologically speaking, this present moment is informed by both past and future. My genetic history is incarnate and my future encoded in my DNA. Each ongoing moment of my organismic life is already shaped by my genetic destiny. Being time-borne, we carry both past and future within every present moment. Our DNA was formed over a millennial past and projects its intentions into the unforeseeable future.

There is a paradoxical phrase I carry around, like a smooth pebble, and rub against my mind to help me make some kind of sense out of my experience of the weird variations of time. "Hope is a memory of the future," Gabriel Marcel said. Could it be that my future has always been present as an encoded promise that draws me forward toward the unfolding of my potential? How much of the promise of what I may become sleeps in my DNA, waiting only to be awakened by the kiss of circumstances? As the great oak tree is already present in the acorn and the seedling, so is my end (my telos) present in my beginning. Premonitions of the future may be brief visions of a destiny that has been encoded in me from the beginning.

The idea of destiny intrigues me. It is a terrible dogma, especially when it is used to deny human freedom, but it points to a powerful experience. In some way we are always who we were and who we are becoming. Human consciousness, like the arc of the trapeze, is always going back and forth between awareness, remembrance, and hope. The pendulum never rests in the dead center of the ever-vanishing present. If we had a clock that measured our inner experience of time, it would not sound the simple cadence of seconds—tick, tock, tick, tock. Rather, it would be the intricate sound: Tick—Once upon a time, Tock—Someday soon, Tick . . . Human beings are time travelers. Our past is not past, nor is our future yet to come.

What was and what will be are crisscrossing the present moment like two flyers doing the "difficult and dangerous passing leap."

Analogies taken from physics and theology give me other tentative handles.

Quantum physics portrays a strange world in which the arrow of time moves backward and forward at the same moment *and* stands still at the speed of light. It even plays with the idea of wormholes in space, and parallel universes.

According to the theistic vision, our past, present, and future are contained within the timeless being of God. As the hymn says, "God of our past, our times are in Thy hand; with us abide. . . . God of the coming years through paths unknown we follow Thee."

It comes down to this for me. None of these metaphors solves the mystery of time. I love the rich and messy experience of time more than any neat theory. I am unwilling to draw religious conclusions from my clock-shattering exceptions to the "normal" sense of time that take place when I enter the magical, mystical time machine or to label them as "illusions." They seem to me to be valuable clues pointing in the direction of metaphysical treasure for which it is worth searching.

Long ago, when I was apple-cheeked and innocent as Adam, I was camping with my father and my brother, Lawrence, somewhere on the Cumberland Plateau in Tennessee. Deep in a remote wilderness littered with rocks of random sizes and shapes, we came upon one rock, seated in the ground, that seemed to be a perfect cube. Curious as to why this symmetrical object should be present in the ordinary chaos of nature, we pushed and pulled until we dislodged it from the ground and turned it bottom side up. To our delight and mystification, there was an arrow cut deeply into the rock pointing in a westerly direction. With flaming curiosity we set off in the indicated direction, tramping back and forth in search of something of significance. Several hundred yards later we came upon a second cubic rock and, excitedly, turned it over. There was another arrow etched in the rock pointing back in the direction of the first rock. We spent many hours that day and the next looking for the hidden treasure—or mystery—to which the two arrows pointed. We never found anything, but to this day we remain convinced that the arrows pointed to something of great significance and we were enriched by our search.

These moments of "sideslipping" and running forward in time are arrows pointing in the direction of the mythic kingdom of freedom and transcendence—the realm from which the flying man came and to which he returns.

CHAPTER 15

On the Wings of Spirit

Sometimes I go about pitying myself. All the time I am being
carried on great winds across the sky.

Chippewa song

My epiphany began in the Sports Bar at the Reno
Hilton on the last night of my second pilgrimage to Reno.

I had come back to Reno to talk with Tony Steele, who by
now had become my major consultant and friend, and to see
the performance of the Flying Cranes—reputedly the greatest
flying act in the world. During the afternoon I attended their
practice session, and on Vilen Golovko's invitation, I joined the
immortals on the pedestal and took a few swings.

I had a couple of hours to kill before the performance
began and I intended to have a beer and return to my room to
escape the cacophony of the casino. But, as I sat in the Sports
Bar nursing my beer, the constant beeping and clanging of the
slot machines and the wall of videos, each showing a different
sporting event, produced a strangely comforting background of
white noise that freed my mind to wander. I settled deeply into
the cushions of a large chair.

I must have slipped into sleep because I awoke with a start
to the sound of wild cheering and applause. For an instant I was
disoriented. Through half-opened eyes I saw blurred images of
horses running neck and neck, and two groups of men locked
in battle. Before I could clarify what was happening, lines from
Matthew Arnold's "Dover Beach" popped into mind:

Learning to Fly

And we are here as on a darkening plain
Swept with confused alarms of struggle and flight
Where ignorant armies clash by night

Forcing my eyes open, I returned to "reality." The phantasm I had been seeing in my semiconscious state was a confused collage from a bank of television screens that was simultaneously showing a boxing match, a horse race, a basketball game, and three football games. The cheering was from a group of enthusiastic fans of the Blue team (maybe the University of Michigan, or the Dallas Cowboys), who had just made a touchdown and were, now, ahead of the Red team (maybe the Redskins). Not being a fan of either team, or of football for that matter, I watched the game from a great aesthetic distance, appreciating the choreographed formations and the graceful movements of the individual players—especially when seen in the slow-motion replays.

Gradually, against my intentions, I found myself being pulled into the game in a partisan way. I knew it was the fourth quarter and the Red team was behind by four points. That made them the underdogs, and that made me want them to win. Suddenly, I was a vicarious warrior with a stake in the outcome of the battle. As the Reds got the ball in the last two minutes and began their tense march downfield, my adrenaline rose and my breathing quickened. As they came out of the huddle for the last play (which had to be a pass, because the clock was ticking off the final seconds), I sat on the edge of my chair. The pass was thrown, the receiver in the end zone jumped high into the air, and . . .

Never mind how the game ended. It is irrelevant. What puzzled me was why I had gotten so involved in a football game. Why was I seduced into caring who won when I didn't even know the names of the teams and I didn't follow the sport?

I still had plenty of time before the evening performance so I decided to meditate on the koan—the mystery of football.

Most meditative traditions recommend the use of some device to focus awareness so the mind can wander freely—allow your eyes to focus lightly on the flame of a candle or chant OM. I chose as my meditative focus the screen that was showing a game between a Green and a Black team. I half-closed my eyes so I would see the contest only as a series of flickering images on the cave wall of my mind and began to free associate as if I were on a therapist's couch or a meditation retreat.

Football. A game. Not like hide-and-seek or jump rope. Not free play. Not, necessarily, fun. It involves two teams, and the object is not to enjoy the game but to win, to upset, quash, triumph over, conquer, overpower, crush, wallop, beat, trounce, defeat the opposition. It absorbs the attention of American audiences and commands near fanatical loyalty from fans. It is "full of sound and fury," but what does it signify?

The central "sport" of any culture is never merely fun, games, and entertainment. Bullfighting, for instance. Football is a public rite, a liturgy performed again and again, a secular sacrament that dramatizes and celebrates the values, philosophy of life, and worldview of a community.

I remembered that Michael Novak—a theologian I knew when we were both young Turks, who went Right when I went Left—had argued that the big three American sports demand that we use images we derive from the male genitalia—balls, getting it up, thrust, holding, driving onward. And they demand that we feel and channel the emotions of hatred, distrust, confidence, humiliation, rage, comradeship, contempt, fear, cunning, joy, and ecstasy. One might think that Novak, being a Christian theologian, would object to the celebration of violence. But no. He takes great delight in being a voyeur of warfare and finds in the ritualized violence that Americans so love a refutation of liberalism. Football is a revelatory liturgy. It externalizes the warfare in our hearts and offers us a means of knowing ourselves and wrestling some grace from our true natures.

No doubt he is correct in his judgment that football is an accurate reflection of the metaphysics and the values of capitalism. But, at this stage in human history should we be celebrating these values? Or questioning them? How many more centuries of the religion of warfare can we abide? How much more competition, winner-take-all, one-upmanship, machismo, can we abide before the whole world resembles Beirut, Vietnam, or Bosnia?

I think Novak either forgot or revised his history to fit his ideology. The Greeks invented the Olympic Games—the noble contest or "agon"—to domesticate our tendency toward violence and to act as a moral equivalent of war. The Games were a public ritual conducted on a consecrated stage and dedicated to reducing the emotions of hatred, distrust, rage, and contempt.

As these thoughts and feelings whirled around my mind, I became aware that my stomach was churning. My ambivalent gut reaction to football, and all that it symbolizes, was enough to give me colon spasms. I dislike ritualized violence *and* I am drawn to it, in the same way I was once both horrified and fascinated by a bullfight I saw in the great ring in Barcelona. Violent rituals show me something about myself and my culture I would rather not see. I am, we are, filled with inner conflicts and addicted to violence. Far from hating violence, we are in love with it. Television is the answer to our prayers: "Give us this day our daily blood, our cop shows, our serial killers, our celebrity murders, our rapes, our visions of mayhem and genocide. And grant us heroes—warriors, fighters, sanctified killers—who will deliver us from evil and preserve our righteous way of life."

I thought about my own darkness—the greed, pettiness,

resentment, and violence that stains the fabric of my being and is not washed away by all my good intentions—and my tendency to make enemies so I will have someone to blame. Then it occurred to me: precisely because we are addicted to warfare we need new games, new public liturgies, new mythic dramas, new sacraments that will give us a vision of courage and daring that is not aimed at conquest.

What symbolic drama would I put in their place if I could erase the old liturgies and retire the phantom warriors who celebrate conflict and violence on the screens of the Sports Bar? What would be an appropriate public liturgy for a society that decided, as the Negro spiritual said, it "ain't going to study war no more"?

Flying trapeze! What better to give us a premonition of what Joachim of Fiore, a twelfth-century monk called "the third age of the spirit," a time in which we would celebrate cooperation rather than competition, lyric virtues rather than the martial vices. In the biblical tradition, the new age of the spirit that Isaiah prophesied was characterized as a time when the ancient habit of violence would be broken. "Instead of the thorn the fig tree; the lion will lie down with the lamb; we will study war no more," and Sunday afternoons will not be given over to the NFL. In that mythic time, "those who wait upon the Lord will mount up with wings as eagles"—and fly.

Because we usually think of trapeze as a form of entertainment in the ambience of the circus, we are unaccustomed to thinking of it as a ceremony that incorporates a message.

What is the gospel according to trapeze, its good news, about the human condition? The artistry of the trapeze troupe emerges from a cooperative effort to create something of fleeting and fragile beauty. It knows danger but not violence, courage but not conquest, striving for excellence but not competition, the joy of achievement but not victory. As a strictly physical achievement the quadruple somersault to the hands of a catcher is a feat of skill, daring, and grace that is unmatched by any ball-bearing athlete in the NBA or NFL.

In this ceremony, at long last, gender really doesn't matter. If some trapeze troupes still have only token female flyers who do simple tricks in skimpy costumes, others like the Korean troupe are predominantly female. In the airborne commonwealth, men and women must submit to the same disciplines, develop the same measure of strength, stamina, and courage, take identical risks to create the ultimate performance art—a drama enacted by a flyer and a catcher on an airy stage that has a life span a million times briefer than a Navajo or Tibetan sand painting, a Christo fence, or a Soho performance. The ephemeral beauty created by a trapeze troupe lasts only a few seconds from the time the flyer leaves the platform, goes to the hands of the catcher, and returns to the platform. Like quarks, those subatomic particles that are released when atoms are bombarded in a cyclotron, the substance of the trapeze art exists for an instant and vanishes forever. We watch with fascination, and then it is over almost before it began, leaving us with an image of fleeting and eternal beauty.

The aerial art celebrates what the poet Wislawa Szymborska called "the passing moment, beautiful beyond belief," that is every man and woman's story.

The performance within the flying theater invites us to remember that we are creatures of earth and air. Like the grass of the field, the wind passes over us and we are gone. Time drags us toward the humus. Yet we are animated by an insistent urge to transcend our limits, to rise up on the wings of hope, to soar.

I was just getting around to imagining a liturgy for a new era when I realized it was nearly time for the Cranes performance. I left the Sports Bar, made my way into the theater, was handed a program and ushered to my seat, and rejoined my companions—Tony Steele and a group of trapeze enthusiasts.

As I read the program of "Aireus" I began to suspect the evening would be a mixed experience. It listed every dancer, understudy, wig maker, wardrobe mistress, and vice president of marketing but did not name any member of the Flying Cranes troupe or tell us anything about its history. The program informed me that the director's trademark "consists of style, class, glitz, and glamour with a unique twist for avant-garde" and warned me that the show had no story line but that it was a fantasy inspired by "Aireus, the ancient Norse goddess of flight, who used to carry out missions for Wotan, the god of war."

This seems at variance with everything I knew about the Flying Cranes. They had worked for seventeen years to create an aerial drama about peace based on a Russian poem about the transformation of the souls of fallen soldiers into white cranes. Their entire performance was designed to tell an antiwar story of death and resurrection.

The houselights dimmed and Aireus began. Strobes and loud, fast music drove the synapses of the brain in the direction of frenzy. Space-helmeted, lycra-clad dancers appeared on different levels of a pipe scaffolding such as one might find on a construction site. Their movements were vaguely menacing, more aggressive than sensuous; their helmeted features suggested a space-age Roman legion. A showgirl costumed as a fantastic white bird of paradise appeared high on the scaffolding and danced her way down to the stage. Two men soared above the audience, the straps around their arms wrapping and unwrapping to vary their height. One act followed another without rhyme or reason. Several dance numbers were indistinguishable except for the change of costume and props—large plastic balls, hula hoops, twirling ribbons, large jacks, wheels.

The entire show conveyed hostility—especially toward women. In an act I would entitle "Aerial Sadomasochism," a showgirl appeared from the ceiling and was pulled in several directions by lines attached to her arms and legs by four male dancers whose painted faces leered like members of a street gang. In what was meant to be a comic parody of "tits and ass," a woman dressed to resemble an overplump stripper or whore sashayed across stage flaunting inflated rubber breasts and buttocks. The only lyrical moment in the show was an adagio number in which two women suspended on wires did a weightless dance, like feathers on the wind, and were twirled by two male dancers.

The applause was, at most, polite. Most of the audience seemed underwhelmed by an hour and a half of this variety show. Members of our group made critical observations and irreverent comments. The women, in particular, smelled misogyny, felt demeaned by the trivialization of women and outraged by the mean-faced male dancers who dominated the female dancers in every act. It was interesting that none of us felt there was anything erotic about the show—so many gyrating bodies, revealing so much flesh and so little tenderness, sensuality, or celebration. There was no sense of communal effort, only individual acts that tried to generate excitement by cacophonous music, fast action, a hint of violence, and a sprinkling of sex.

It occurred to me that Aireus was the second half of the symbolic rite of warfare I had been watching earlier in the Sports Bar—the nightclub version of the Dallas Cowboys cheerleaders. In the warrior's vision of the world, all that is feminine—soft, sensuous, nurturing, kindly—is subjected to the control of what is "manly"—aggressive, dominating, conquering, tough. As Nietzsche said, when the warrior goes to a woman, he takes a whip. Whether consciously or unconsciously, the "creative team" of Aireus kidnapped the goddess and forced her to carry out missions for Wotan, the god of war.

At long last, the Flying Cranes arrived.

The stage grew dark and was filled with mist; everything was suffused with a soft light. In the milky light of dawn, we saw a net suspended above the stage and two white-clad luminescent figures that might have been large birds or ballet dancers perched on a bar high in the air.

Suddenly, there was a clap of thunder and a flash of lightning, and one of the Cranes, Elena Golovko, the only woman in the act—identified in the original Russian version as the last of the fallen soldiers—fell gracefully from a great height to the net, writhed, ran, and jumped like a springbok that had been injured. Four Cranes appeared from somewhere in the surrounding darkness and ascended rapidly, pulled into the upper regions by invisible cords. In the gathering light, we saw that there were other figures, almost like angels, perched in the shadows.

The light changed from suffused white to crisscrossed shafts of red, blue, and gold, reminding me of a display of northern lights. Two Cranes descended on invisible wires, swung back and forth, joined hands, whirled together, and cradled their fallen comrade between them. A third Crane descended, hanging by his knees from a bar, and the three carried their comrade Elena upward. When they had ascended nearly out of view of the audience, she fell to the net and her fellow Cranes descended and lifted her once again. This drama of the fallen soul and the community that bears it heavenward was accompanied by swelling strains of the romantic music of Stravinsky, Tchaikovsky, Wagner, with some Bach, Liszt, and Ravel.

The mood changed. The entire set was brightly illuminated

and we saw a company of Cranes perched on various pedestals. The catcher began to swing in his rhythmic arc and the trapeze performance began. Right from the beginning, I was aware that it resembled nothing I had ever seen before and that it was going to be impossible to describe. It was less like a traditional trapeze troupe than an exhalation of skylarking flyers—a flock of birds frolicking in midair. One flyer took off from the pedestal and soared so high, turning in a double layout, that he was practically lost in space before he descended to the hands of the catcher. Other Cranes initiated their flight from the opposite end of the rig, from two high trapezes and perches that were at the center, or from the Russian swing that also served as the catcher's cradle. You never quite knew where a flyer would appear from or where he would go. Just when you thought he would fly from the hands of the catcher to a waiting trapeze, he flew straight up to the hands of a second catcher. And once airborne, the flyers traveled enormous distances before reaching the hands of a catcher or another waiting trapeze. When a flyer fell, he danced on the net, held one arm high, grasped a waiting cable, and was lifted back up to the pedestal so gracefully that it was clear to the audience that falls were planned for and made beautiful even when unintentional.

There was a moment when Elena Golovko did a splits and dropped to the hands of catcher. The move itself was so simple it could be done by any flexible fledgling, but she executed it with such exquisite slowness and fluidity that she stole the audience's breath away. In that instant, flesh and blood was transubstantiated and she became the essence of each person's inner vision of transcendent beauty. For me she was sunlight streaming through a cascade of honey, the flute song of a wood thrush just before twilight.

There is at least a partial explanation for the seemingly metaphysical flight of the Cranes. They remain aloft longer than most flyers because their rig is considerably larger than the standard circus rig. Their trapezes are hung on fourteen-foot rather than the twelve-foot cables; their catcher's cradle is suspended from ten-foot rather than eight-foot cables and is three feet lower than normal; the distance between the flyer and the catcher is thirty feet rather than the standard twenty-five. All of this allows a flyer to swing higher, fly further, and remain longer in the air before reaching the hands of the catcher. In addition, they make use of electrically winched cables (levitors) that hoist flyers aloft and let them swing back and forth at any level.

Something Juan Vazquez told me, while not exactly true, is interesting. Comparing the Flying Vazquez and the Flying Cranes he said, "We do the classical flying trapeze. They have good choreography, but they don't do hard tricks." Without question, Miguel Vazquez is one of the most beautiful flyers who has ever lived, and he has done every trick in the book. But nobody would argue seriously that the tricks the Cranes do—double layouts, double layouts with a full twist, double cutaways with one-and-a-half twist, triples, and quadruple somersaults—are easy tricks. To say nothing of the quintuple somersault that Serge Beloujenkov has completed in practice. There is a whole bag of traditional tricks they do not perform—full twisting triples, triples and a half, legs catches, over-the-bar tricks, hocks doubles, pirouette returns, or passing leaps—but Vilen Golovko himself says "our act is not a series of tricks."

The Cranes do not try to dazzle their audiences with pyrotechnics because their performance is more about vision than entertainment, more about soul than style. I think back to something Vilen told me earlier: "The idea of flying is connected to the idea of eternity." Or what Elena said: "You are not just doing tricks. You have to come from your interior, your heart. You are performing a story about the meaning of life. You start with the idea of birth, death, and tragedy, and the realization that people help each other. People are not forgotten. We are not alone in our little boxes. People all around the world have lived and suffered. The climax of the Cranes performance, like life itself, is the ascension; something is transformed if you have the courage to go through life and get its true meaning.''

In part, this accounts for the state of astonishment and enchantment evoked in the audience the moment the performance began. In making the transition from Aireus to the Cranes, the audience was transported from the corner of Hollywood and Vine to an ancient forest of towering redwoods, or a cathedral. It was hushed by the initial drama of the fallen Crane lifted heavenward. When the first flyer soared, people held their breath, and when he reached the hands of the catcher an eternity later, there was a collective sigh of relief and spontaneous applause.

We were moved by the Cranes because what we witnessed was a performance that took place on both a physical and a metaphysical level, a vision of perfection. Every flyer incarnates perfect form—never a dangling leg, an arm out of place, an awkward movement. We saw but were unable to believe what we saw. We heard the clock strike thirteen but knew that was impossible. Human beings are incapable of such flight, such perfection. When a flyer failed to make contact with the catcher and fell to the net, the audience gasped. When he landed safely, we all applauded, relieved by the display of imperfection because the vision of perfection in any art tempts us to disdain our own imperfection.

But having said all this, I find that my words keep collapsing around me like walls of sand when I try to describe the Cranes performance. Mystics returning from an experience of union with what they variously call God, the Buddha mind, the Elan Vital, the Ground of Being, inevitably tell us that the experience is ineffable. You can walk around it with language but cannot describe it accurately. The best I can do to describe this phenomenon is use the old *via negativa* of the mystics and describe what it was *not*. Then, perhaps I can edge closer to the experience by using metaphors.

It wasn't circus. There was no drumroll, no um-pa-pa um-pa-pa. There was no hype about the "greatest, the most difficult, the one and only." There was no star of the show. There was no announcement that we were about to see some legendary, dangerous, or death-defying trick. There was no styling or waiting for applause.

On what needles am I to knit this experience? If it does not belong within the category of circus, or show business, or theater, what is it? Among other things it is an aerial adagio; an epiphany of the fourth dimension in which we catch a glimpse of impossible possibilities, like the disappearing interstices in an Escher drawing or the counterpoint in a Bach fugue; a drama of death and resurrection that reminded me of the moment of initiation in the Eleusinian mystery cult when the priest and priestess descended into a dark place and displayed to the communicants an ear of corn, the sacred symbol of the goddess Demeter.

As I watched the performance, one particular moment became numinous for me, charged with a supernormal significance I could not immediately decipher. The trick itself was as ordinary as bread and wine—a flyer makes a straight jump across a measureless void to the arms of the catcher. It is such a basic trick that even I have completed it more than once, albeit awkwardly. Without warning, something happened that left me dumb with wonder. The flyer, having left the trapeze, never reached the catcher but soared into that endless inner space I can only call my "soul" and remained freeze-framed in mid-leap. I began to weep silently without understanding why. Then, I realized that the Flying Crane soaring through time and space had fused with the timeless image of the flying man that had been with me since that moment he first appeared a lifetime ago, when my father took me to the circus. And I, like all who inhabit the mystery of fleeting time, am a bird that flies from the darkness into a brightly lit room and back into the darkness. I know I may never reach the arms of the catcher, may never know the perfection of unconditional love and acceptance, but I leap again and again into the void with reaching arms and am sustained by hope.

I hardly remember the ending, either of the performance or of the evening. The moment the curtain dropped and the lights went on, I left the theater and returned to my room to mull over the events of the day. A hot bath and a brandy later, I crawled into bed and allowed the images and feelings from the day to run through my mind until I fell asleep and slipped into an elaborate dream.

As the dreams opens, I am in a large domed room that seems to be a combination of a cathedral and a mystery theater. At first glance, the dome appears to be the vault of heaven, filled with stars and constellations clustered in patterns that suggest the signs of the zodiac. As I look more closely, the stars fade and I see that the dome is, like the Sistine Chapel, covered with an elaborate collage of painted figures, a Disneyland rendition of a veritable pantheon of aerial spirits. It resembles the lush display of icons of saints and bodhisattvas I have seen in Buddhist temples in Bhutan. At the very center of the collage, Michelangelo's bearded God is handing Adam a trapeze. Loosely arranged around this central figure, seated together like the apostles in the traditional stained-glass windows of the Last Supper, is a group of the great flyers from different eras. Léotard is wearing his frilled tights, Cadona is doing his signature hand-waving pose, Tony Steele, Fay Alexander, Reggie Armor, Tito Gaona are huddled together, and Miguel Vazquez is using his hands to explain something to them. The Flying Crane-Man I encountered earlier in the evening has his arms lifted above the group as if giving a benediction. Moving out from the center, I see a whole potpourri of creatures that fly or have been imagined to fly or who inhabit the heavenly realms. There are half-bird half-human harpies and delicate winged fairies. Jesus is being lifted up onto a high mountaintop. Saint Paul is ascending, supposedly toward the seventh heaven. Padmasambhava, the great Buddhist saint, is flying on the back of a tiger. Various shamans dressed in animal skins or cloaks of feathers are flying around. Near the bottom of the heavenly vault, a motley assortment of angels are fiddling with their wings and trying to gather the courage to leap into time and gravity and attempt wingless flight, knowing that they can taste the glories of the earth only if they share the human risk of falling. Sprinkled throughout this entire collage are a host of figures I can only describe as archetypes, a museum of perfect specimens of animals—tigers, horses, goats, and birds. I recognize the wood thrush and indigo bunting I loved as a child in the College Woods.

The lush variety of this aerial kingdom baffles me. What has this "overworld" to do with me? As I am trying to puzzle out the significance of all these ethereal, lighter-than-air heavenly beings, I notice that beneath the dome, midway to the floor, is stretched a gossamer trapeze net of spider-woven silk. A variety of ropes and trapezes, some wide enough to hold several people, are suspended from invisible supports.

As my eyes travel further downward the light grows dim and when I reach floor level, I am engulfed in heavy darkness. I am suddenly charged with an air of expectancy and realize that the panorama I have been observing is the setting for my initiation into the Mystery.

In the darkness beneath the net something is stirring. All I can make out is vague outlines, undulating chthonic figures in a sea of dense clay, something moving beneath a blanket of primordial night. Gradually, the lumps become black-clad human figures reaching upward toward the light and then falling back into the darkness. A group of dancers dressed in varying shades of earthen brown and green break away from the mass and strive to ascend. One dancer dressed in red makes her way to the center where a golden rope leads up into the aerial kingdom of the Dome. As she begins to climb, the chthonic forces, rumbling like an earthquake, try to pull her downward. Gradually she escapes their grasp and climbs upward and falls into the spiderweb net.

After resting for a while, she begins a drunken walk around the net. As she falls and bounces, she starts to experiment with the new elastic ground and before long she is leaping and laughing each time she becomes airborne, turning awkward flips like a novice on a trampoline. She goes to the edge of the net, calls to her former companions, shows them the golden thread, and welcomes them into the new realm where they all cavort and play.

The most adventurous of the group finds her way back to the thread and, ignoring the warnings of her fellows, climbs higher until she reaches one of the single trapezes hanging above the net. A spotlight shines on her as she explores the possibilities of the new realm. She begins to swing, hang by her knees, twine herself around the ropes, and gradually creates an aerial dance like that of the great Russian swinging-trapeze artist Elana Panov. As her pendulum approaches an arc of 180 degrees, a spotlight reveals a second figure emerging from the darkness—a catcher swinging from an adjacent trapeze. Our solitary artist swings toward him; their arcs get closer; they try to touch, but cannot, and she falls to the net. The light dims, and darkness descends.

When the light returns, it is like dawn on a soft morning and I can see an entire flying-trapeze troupe made up of an unlikely assortment of tall and short, thin and fat, young and old people perched on various pedestals. Their initial moves are awkward and dangerous. They swing out of control, bump into each other, crash into the pedestal (like I did at Circus-Circus), and fall flailing into the net. There is an almost comic feeling of fledglings, small birds who flap their wings, make clumsy short flights that often end in disaster.

Gradually the flyers lengthen their arcs. They reach out for the catcher but touch only briefly and tentatively. Finally, a flyer manages to hang by his knees and grasp the hands of the catcher, but he refuses to let go, and the catcher drops him into the net. After much experimentation a flyer discovers the plange position and takes the leap of faith across the void to the waiting hands of the catcher.

After this, the airborne troupe cavort and play and create a complex choreography of straight jumps, layouts, double and triple somersaults, and passing leaps.

I am enjoying the performance when I hear a small voice addressing me from the darkness: "Sam, the time has come for you to fly." I turn and see the Flying Crane-Man. He is beckoning me. My hands sweat; I rise from my seat and walk over to the golden thread. I look up toward the Dome and the trapeze rig and begin to climb hand over hand.

Just then I wake up. I am so charged with excitement and a sense of the uncanny that I don't know where I am. When I realize I am in a hotel room in the Reno Hilton, I am disappointed. I don't want to leave the magic aerial theater before I have a chance to perform my small tricks and make a gift of my art to the great audience before whom my life has been performed.

I lie still in my bed and allow myself to sink into the fertile hypnagogic state between waking and sleeping. With my inner eye still focused on the images from the dream, I begin the quest for understanding. What is the dream telling me? I do not usually have such wide-screen Technicolor extravaganzas with a cast of thousands. This spectacle is a metaphysical aerial circus, a mystical theater in which a cosmic drama is being performed and I have a part to play. It is also an elaborate answer to the question I posed to myself earlier in the evening. My dream has presented me with an enacted vision, a ceremony celebrating the primordial, perennial struggle to transcend the forces of gravity that pull us downward, to ascend on the wings of spirit. This is the liturgy for a new era I was seeking—the ultimate context wherein I find the meaning of my passion for flying.

It is, I realize, also a very old story, which has been told in one way or another by every religion and every philosophical idealism. The heavenly Dome is the realm of the ideals, the mind of God, the eternal storage vault of archetypes and laws that bring sweet meaningful order out of chaos, the source of DNA that informs the cosmic process, the indwelling cosmic eros that calls forth our longing and hope for a "higher" way of life.

My dream seemed a kind of reenactment of the myth Plato created in the *Phaedrus*. According to Plato, before we were born, the gods took the soul on a tour round the whole compass of the heavens so it might have a vision of the archetypes of perfect beauty, goodness, and truth to guide it throughout its journey in time. *The goal of human life is for the soul to recover its wings.* If we strive to remember our divine origin, each time we see something of earthly beauty it will trigger our recollection of the perfect goodness, beauty, and truth we glimpsed when the soul was conducted on the great procession by the gods. My vision of the heavenly vault was tailor-made, filled with the images of the aerial heroes who had inspired me.

I feel within myself the opposition between the world of the heavenly dome and the chthonic world of darkness inhabited by those writhing creatures under the net. Something pulls us downward. The dark side of the Force seduces us into unconsciousness, fear, grasping, and conformity. There is a lurking energy that depresses and clips our wings. Some cosmic rogue cop enforces the laws of thermodynamics and gravity that perversely drive us back toward the primal chaos and conspire to bring us low. Something entwined in the heart of matter does not love levity.

The trapeze rig is the realm of time, which, as Plato said, is "the moving image of eternity." As the flyers etch the eternity sign in space with their movements, they discover the balance between gravity and levity and use it to create a communal work of art, to do tricks of transient and eternal beauty.

At the center of this intricate vision, and for me the heart of the epiphany, is the image of the Flying Crane-Man.

What I struggle to understand and stutter to describe has reduced better writers than myself to silence. But, as E. B. White said, "A writer, like an acrobat, must occasionally try a stunt that is too much for him." It is always an ordinary event that becomes transparent to the great mystery—"a flower in a crannied wall"—"a tiger, tiger burning bright in the forest of the night"—the birth of a divine child, which is to say, any child.

Each time the flying man has appeared to me, I have felt a shock of recognition. He comes to me as someone I have always known. He seems to be my personal icon, my individualized archetype, an incarnate symbol of the metaphysical, meta-temporal reality of my self that I might call my essence, my destiny, my soul, or the DNA that has programed, does, and will continue to program my aspirations. He is a seed that was planted in the depths of my self before I had consciousness or choice, a symbol of the fulfillment toward which I have been moving all my life.

Since my earliest awareness, I have felt an unname-able force drawing and pushing me to become airborne, to soar, to escape from rigid habits of mind, to fly free. Something older than the psyche, wiser than the mind, more inventive than the imagination impels and invites each of us to become who we are meant to be. My life has been guided by a star in my inner firmament, by an endarkened vision of certain great ideals. It is as if I recollect, aspire after, and continually fall short of an impossible but necessary ideal of goodness, justice, beauty, and truth. That I have fallen more often than soared is a testimony to the brokenness of the human condition. I do not despair, because the gesture that gives my life dignity and joy is not the execution of a perfect trick. As a dear friend said, "Sam, your performance on the trapeze is like the talking dog—the marvel isn't that he talks well but that he talks at all."

We can only hope that the impulse to transcend, the yearning to be conscious and free, that has brought us this far along the evolutionary path still sleeps in the human DNA and will continue to be the prime mover of our future destiny. There is only one dream that is worthy of the promise encoded in our genes and in the stars, only one vision that inspired our souls in their once-upon-a-time-and-forever-after tour through the circuit of the heavens, and that dream is of a community willing to dedicate itself to making its cities beautiful, its citizens truthful, compassionate, and just, and its landscape fit for the consortium of all life. Should we fail to invest our substance in this dream, we will be condemned by the logic of our delusion to the nightmare of a future governed by "confused alarms of struggle and flight where ignorant armies clash by night" with ever more diabolical clever weapons of mass destruction. The choice we face at this historical crossroad is whether the governing image of the future will be the warrior or the flying man.

If there is to be a politics of compassion, we must allow the dis-graceful ceremonies of violence to die out and be replaced by the vision of an airborne community struggling to be reborn, risking its life to soar on the wings of the spirit.

CHAPTER 16

Give Us This Day

The flying act is one you do with your heart. It is our daily bread.
Every time you eat it you enjoy it.

Ruben Caballero Jr.

Mountaintops are *great* places to visit but not to live. My peak experience in Reno, my encounter with the Flying Crane-Man, and my dream gave me a deeper understanding of my strange passion for trapeze. But when the morning dawned, I was happy to pack up my dream and head for home and the familiar routine of daily practice with my friends in the Sonoma Trapeze Troupe.

In recounting the experience of those revelatory moments when we suddenly see what was long obscured, when a brief epiphany shifts our understanding of self and world, there is a temptation to cast the story in the form of the traditional religious miracle tale. But mine was no conversion on the Damascus Road or sudden enlightenment under the Bo Tree. At best, when I returned home I experienced a loss of ambition and a deeper acceptance of the sweet imperfection of daily life.

There are moments when I find myself adding up my meager repertoire of tricks and making an "objective" judgment about the results of my years of practice. Then I am embarrassed in my own eyes—so much effort for so little result—just as I am embarrassed when people ask me exactly what tricks I have perfected. Can you do a somersault? A double? A suicide

to the net? A passing leap? Have you become a master of catching, compassion, and care?

Truth told, my bag of tricks is small and there are days
when I become discouraged. I wish I could tell you a heroic
story—I started as a bumbling mass of quivering jelly but have
learned, after many trials and tribulations, to throw a perfectly
coordinated and confident triple somersault. Alas, I remain a
perpetual fledgling. But there are days when some kindly wind
blows through the trees, cooling my hot hands, turning the net
into an aeolian harp, and I remember my greatest achievement—I love to practice. I am a true amateur.

Of course, being an amateur has nothing to do with one's
level of skill or whether one is paid for performing. Recently I
interviewed two world-famous flyers; one has remained an enthusiastic amateur, the other has become a highly accomplished
professional. I met the amateur—Luiz Caballero—in his trailer
after his performance at Ringling Brothers Circus. He and his
family, all of whom are trapeze artists, live and breathe their
art. They explain that they still practice every day and are
working on several new tricks. "There are days," he tells me,
"when my hands hurt and I'm tired and I don't want to practice and then, for a little while, I hate the trapeze. But flying is
in my blood; it's not just something I do. I love it." It is easy to
see by the animation in his face that he means it. The other
flyer, whom I will not name, performs his act with unbelievable
ease and breathtaking skill, but there is no sparkle in his eye, no
blush of joy. He has accomplished his goals so he has ceased to
practice.

The disease of professionalism that infects teachers, physi-
cians, and lawyers, no less than flyers, begins when goals become more important than process, when practice becomes a
means rather than a source of enjoyment. Focusing on a distant
goal, we never cherish the moment. We mortgage the present
to make a down payment on a future that keeps receding.

The great trick is to make the pleasure of living each day our most important "goal." We would do well to jettison the Western, secular myth of progress and adopt the official maxim that graces the postage stamps of the gentle Buddhist kingdom of Bhutan—"Gross National Happiness."

My now and future miracle is not the triple, but the enjoyment I get when I point my toes, smile, swing with all the strength and verve I possess, and hope for the grace that will make my brief trick a thing of beauty.

The perfect practice is one that does not depend on practice making perfect. Practice *is* perfect.

I do not deny that I continue to make improvement in mastering the art. But this is not the point. At the deepest level the practice is about making a gesture, performing a symbolic act, enacting a sacrament. What is important is not the observable trick but what happens *within* the flyer—the metaphysical flight through inner space.

Learning how to make the right gestures is an important skill. Any simple movement can be transformed into a gesture that symbolizes a basic attitude, stance, or feeling we have about our life. Every religious tradition has a rich repertoire of gestures, mudras, and symbolic acts that embody faith—hands clasped in prayer, bowing toward Mecca, kneeling before the altar, dervish dances.

To remain alive and vital we must be able to swing back and forth between seeming opposites. We humans are complex beings who contain many contradictions.

We are hyphenated beings—meta-physical, or metamorphic animals. We are body and . . . something more. One great question has haunted us since that prehistorical moment when we first emerged into self-consciousness: What is this something more, this metaphysical mystery, this beyond-within that always beckons us? The great words *spirit, soul,* and *mind* are merely ways of pointing to the something more—the *meta*—that is part of our hyphenated identity.

My quest is not to arrive at some definitive knowledge of the complexities of who I am, but to cherish the mystery of my inspired flesh. It is to remember that I, like a proton, am a paradoxical, hyphenated, quantum being. At once I am:

> *solitary self* . . . . *communal being*
> *single atom-particle* . . . . *event-wave*
> *physical body* . . . . . . *metaphysical "spirit"*
> *being* . . . . *ground of Being*
> *historical person* . . . . . *transcender of time*
> *earthbound* . . . . *airborne*

Because we so easily forget, we need some practice to prompt our awareness of our marvelous complexity. It hardly matters what we choose as a vehicle for our liturgies of remembrance. Pick any mundane activity and convert it into a metaphysical gesture, an outward and visible sign of an inward and invisible grace. Take bread and wine and imagine it to be the body of God. Take tea and cakes and become enlightened. Arrange flowers and create your world. Raise a child. Practice healing. Choose your place to explore the beyond-within. Walk, ski, surf, golf, dream, cook, love, breathe, dance, or fly as a contemplative practice.

Any church, woods, bedroom, boardroom, or playing field may become consecrated ground. The other day, Tony Steele reported to me that when he looked over at the trapeze grounds across the creek there seemed to be a halo around it. "I think we should adopt the custom used in Karate schools," he said. "They bow before they go onto the mat. We should bow before we go across the bridge onto the trapeze ground."

The body is a sacramental site, a place of revelation. The apocalypse is here and now. Flesh is a sacred text that must be deciphered. Our metaphoric practice, our personal sacrament, is the place of apocalypse, metamorphosis, and revolution. It is the quantum crossroads where I meet that stranger who is myself—and more.

Howard Thurman once confided in me when he was in his eighties and not in good health, "The hard thing when you get old is to keep your horizons open. The first part of your life everything is in front of you, all your potential and promise. But over the years, you make decisions, you carve yourself into a given shape. Then the challenge is to keep discovering the green growing edge."

The only way I know to resist the perennial temptation to slip into routine and sacrifice my spirit to yesterday's gods is to keep the sight and sensation of the edge. If I am not careful, the kingdom I have created by imagination and hard work becomes my prison. Help! I'm caught in the ego I constructed brick by brick.

Yesterday, I spent an hour practicing my face-off falls to the net. The movement, or form, I was trying to perfect is similar to what a diver does in executing a swan dive. I wanted to fall with my body parallel to the net, my arms stretched wide, my feet together, and at the last moment, tuck an arm, twist, and land on my back. The move frightens me because I feel I don't have enough time both to open fully and make the necessary rotation. Consequently, I have gotten in the bad habit of remaining half-closed and turning prematurely with my legs flailing.

It had been raining for several days and I was especially eager to practice. Since my verve factor was high, I decided to try an experiment. I put some strong rubber bands around my ankles to force me to keep my feet together. About the third attempt everything clicked. With swan wings and feet extended into a narrow point, I hovered above the net for a leisurely instant before cat-turning to my back. In that instant I was once again and forever a winged creature, free from the bondage of time and gravity.

Today, I am enlivened by a sense of new possibilities. I feel a kind of visceral hope as if some underground spring has come to the surface. There is always something new and refreshing ready to bud in the dark recesses of the self. We are filled with seeds—potentialities, promises, talents—that lie dormant for half a lifetime waiting for the right time to germinate. When we become dry and brittle, we have only to cultivate the hint of emerald that first appears on the edge.

The edge is the "thin, sharpened side, as of the blade of a cutting instrument. A penetrating, incisive quality. Keenness, as of desire or enjoyment; zest. The line of intersection of two surfaces. A rim or brink. The area or part away from the middle; an extremity. A dividing line; a border. A point of transition." *(Webster's Third New International Dictionary)*

As a place to live, the edge combines risk and promise, fear and desire. It is the place of openness to what is new, willingness to expand our sense of the possible, a place where the ego is constantly dying and being reborn, where constriction gives way to inspiration. It cannot be inhabited with bravado or defiance. Nor can it be conquered. It is the vernal dwelling place of that divine creativity that drives us to become who we are.

It is time for me to bring this meditation on the art of flying to a close.

I have told this tale as if it had a beginning and an end. But everything that appears to our horizon-bound eyes as linear really curves and heads back toward home. We are born and we die but something in us goes round and round again. If I look into the depths from which I came, I may see that yesterday and today and tomorrow are not so separate as they seem. We always seem to be beginning again even though there is some-thing in us that neither begins nor ends.

I know that the great lessons and simple truths I have learned in my struggle to live with passion, compassion, and wisdom will have to be relearned. I expect to be wrestling with fear, greed, and illusion so long as I choose to remain aware of my twisted ways and search for a more gracious manner of life. The life-curriculum does not begin with Elementary Facts 101 and proceed in an orderly way to Advanced Wisdom 505 and Absolute Enlightenment 909. No one gains mastery of the art of living without much backsliding and circuitous wanderings.

The Great Path is a spiral journey. Round and round we go, as in the legendary triple somersault, until, in the words of the Shaker hymn, "by turning, turning we come round right." Every day we begin again, knowing that danger and death may be lurking, that we will be fearful and will need to cultivate courage. We will need to keep our balance and discern when it is time to wait and when to act. We will take leaps of faith, fall, and rise again. If we are diligent in our practice, there will be unexpected moments of grace and joy and a gradual growth of mastery in fashioning our lives into something of beauty.

ACKNOWLEDGMENTS

During the last five years, my practice of the flying trapeze has introduced me to a community and a living group of heroes and heroines. I have attended every circus I could find from Ringling Brothers to traveling "mud shows." I have frequented the Circus-Circus Casinos in Las Vegas and Reno, which for more than thirty years have featured famous trapeze artists. I have visited the Wenatchee Youth Circus and the Peru Youth Circus. I took my family on a working vacation to Club Med, which spawned the present amateur movement, and to the Festival of the Circus of Tomorrow at the Cirque de Hivre in Paris. In all these places I interviewed flyers and catchers to collect the stories, lore, and traditions of the aerial world. Often I was invited to share a practice session and have, with much trepidation, done my small tricks in the company of some of the greatest trapeze artists of our time. Like an anthropologist who has "gone native," I went out as an observer and ended up a member of a marvelous tribe.

I want to thank all the troupes I visited, the flyers, catchers, and special informants I interviewed: the Flying Vazquez, the Flying Gaonas, the Flying Cranes, the Flying Vargas, the Flying Pages, the Flying Poemas, the Flying Caballeros, the Flying Kaganovitch, the Flying Rodogels, Tito Richie Armando and Chela Gaona, Vilen and Elena Golovko, Peter Gold, Ray Valentine Jr., Bob Yerkes, Fay and Rose Alexander, Terri and Jim Caveretta, Reggie Armor, Harry Graham, Dominic Jando (aerial director for Big Apple Circus), and Jan Roc Achard (Ecole Nationale de Cirque). Special thanks to my heavyweight agent and friend Ned Leavitt who flew to me and was caught, thus avoiding the dreaded headline, "Author Drops Agent." Finally, give my regards to Broadway, to everyone who believed in this book and helped it fly.

There are very few written accounts of the history of trapeze and most of these are in obscure circus publications. The most helpful of those available are:

Steve Gossard, *A Reckless Era of Aerial Performance: The Evolution of Trapeze.* Self-published, available from the author: Curator of Circus Collections, 10 Siesta Court, Bloomington, IL 61704.

Harry Graham, *Born to Fly: The Story of Tito Gaona* and *The Biggest Trick: Miguel Vazquez' Quadruple Somersault.* Both published by Words and Pictures Press, P.O. Box 6623, Orange, CA 92613.

The ABCs of Trapeze, a manual describing how to do various tricks is available from the author Tony Steele, 145 Grove St., #23, Reno, NV 89502 for $15.00.

Should you be interested in learning the flying trapeze, you can find a complete list of trapeze rigs and schools at High Flying Trapeze Resource Page at:

www.damnhot.com/trapeze;

for e-mail, try Trapeze@damnhot.com;

for Web-related info, e-mail to ludwig@damnhot.com;

for information about programs conducted by Sonoma Trapeze Troupe, write to 16331 Norrbom Rd., Sonoma, CA 95476.